THE INDEPENDENT GUIDE TO NEW YORK CITY (3RD EDITION)

HANNAH BORENSTEIN (AUTHOR)

AND

G. COSTA (EDITOR)

Limit of Liability and Disclaimer of Warranty:
The publisher has used its best efforts in preparing this book, and the information provided herein is provided "as is." Independent Guides and the author make no representation or warranties with respect to the accuracy or completeness of the contents of this book and specifically disclaims any implied warranties of merchantability or fitness for any particular purpose and shall in no event be liable for any loss of profit or any other commercial damage, including but not limited to special, incidental, consequential, or other damages.

Please read all safety information at attractions, dining locations and accommodation providers, as well as the terms and conditions of any third party companies used. Prices are approximate, and do fluctuate.

Copyright Notice:
Contents copyright (C) 2012-2018 Independent Guides. All rights reserved. No part of this document or the related files may be reproduced or transmitted in any form, by any means (electronic, photocopying, recording, or otherwise) without the prior written permission of the publisher, unless it is for personal use.

Contents

1: New York City: A Brief History	**4**
2: NYC: Know Before You Go	**6**
Internet Access	7
Currency	7
Weather	8
Typical NYC Food	8
NYC Customs and Etiquette	9
3: Getting to NYC	**10**
4: Transportation in NYC	**12**
5: Top 10 Attractions	**16**
6: Neighbourhood Guides	**18**
Harlem	20
Upper West Side	24
Upper East Side	29
Midtown	32
Chelsea	39
Flatiron	43
Gramercy Park	45
Union Square	48
Greenwich Village	50
West Village	54
East Village	57
SoHo/NoLita	61
Lower East Side	64
Tribeca	68
Chinatown	70
Little Italy	72
Financial District	73
Brooklyn	78
Queens	82
The Bronx	86
Staten Island	89
7: Shopping	**92**
8: Nightlife	**96**
Bars/Lounges/Pubs/Clubs	96
Live Music	98
Theater	99
9: Seasonal Events	**101**
10: Maps	**106**

New York City: A Brief History

In order to understand how New York City has become the 24-hour city it is today, it is worth looking back to see how the 'Big Apple' evolved.

European Settlement

The *Lenape* Native American tribe, which means "genuine, pure, and original", ruled the territory along the Delaware River, including parts of modern day Delaware, New Jersey, Pennsylvania, and the area that is now New York City.

Settlers first came to the island of Manhattan in 1609. That year, Englishman Henry Hudson sailed a Dutch East India Company ship, the Half Moon, to the tip of the island. Within a decade, the Dutch West Indian Company was sending African slaves to construct the settlements, including protection from the Native American inhabitants. In 1647, the Dutch were granted power over what they then called "New Amsterdam".

There was a huge amount of development including building a protective wall (now Wall Street), a canal into the island (now Broad Street) and the foundations of Broadway. However, by 1667, the English seized the land and renamed it "New York" after the Duke of York.

For the century that followed leading up to the Revolutionary War, African slaves were a significant part of the population. Today, in Lower Manhattan the African Burial Ground Monument remembers this period.

Post American Revolution

As the Continental Army fought against British troops following the Declaration of Independence, New York was witness to its fair share of bloodshed. It was not until 1783 that the British forces ultimately left the city and shortly after, New York was considered the capital of the United States.

As the 1840s rolled around, NYC began establishing itself as an immigrant city. First the Great Irish Famine brought large numbers of Irish immigrants to New York, and then the Civil War victory and the emancipation of slaves gave New York the image of immigrant opportunities.

The Statue of Liberty was given as a gift by French sculptor Frederic Augeste Bartholdi, which was to be a representation of freedom and liberty to those moving to the United States of America.

At the turn of the 20th century, NYC started experiencing rapid and modernizing industrialization. Pennsylvania Station followed Grand Central Terminal's successful opening, as did the Interborough Rapid Transit (NYC's first subway company).

Additionally, some of the most iconic skyscrapers began to appear, including the Flatiron Building in 1902 and the Woolworth Building in 1913 (the tallest building in the world until 1930).

Throughout the 1920s and 1940s NYC changed, grew, and flourished. United States minority migrants, as well as international immigrants, fled to New York in droves. This led to NYC becoming a hub for manufacturing and industrialization. Immigrants brought with them their learned trades and upon arriving created garments, jewelry, and various other products to support themselves.

Despite the Great Depression, the city continued to build – the Chrysler building and the Empire State Building were constructed in 1931 and various other significant buildings followed.

Post World War II

The demographics and population numbers changed greatly during World War II, and the years following the war were met with uncertainty and alterations.

NYC, though seen as a leading city worldwide, was transitioning from its industrial history toward the financial, commercial, and corporate sectors.

The civil rights movements, gang wars, and bohemian movement, brought crime, drugs, and poverty to NYC during the 1970s and 1980s. In 1975, the island found itself close to bankruptcy and the majority of neighborhoods were deemed unsafe to walk through.

As the city slowly got back on its feet with effects from the 'dot com' boom and government-funded restoration projects, it began to transform into the identity it maintains today – safer, yet still colored with diversity.

The City Today

New York City continues to experience substantial changes. The attacks of September 11, 2001 caused devastation to both the physical city, and the morale of its citizens, as did the more recent Hurricane Sandy in 2012.

However, the city has continued to preserve its iconic appeal.

Today, New York City is the most populated city in the United States. As of 2018, there were about 8.6 million residents. With the small geographic space of NYC, this means that the average density is just fewer than 28,000 people per square mile.

In the next few chapters, we cover the essential information you need to visit New York City today.

Chapter Two | Know Before You Go

NYC: Know Before You Go

Before we start uncovering the delights of New York City, we will take a brief look at information you should know before you arrive.

The Local Population

NYC remains the most densely populated city in the United States, and is often considered on of the most diverse cities on the planet.

With about 8.6 million residents, NYC has more locals than Los Angeles and Chicago combined. In 2010, the city's population was approximately 44% white, 25% black, 29% hispanic, and 13% asian. This does not add up to 100% as some people identify themselves as being of multiple races.

Since the turn of the 20th century when the term "melting pot" was created to refer to the immigrant neighborhoods of Lower Manhattan, diversity has manifested and maintained itself through cultural, religious, and ethnic enclaves, scattered throughout.

Although some groups have moved due to gentrification, some of the largest populations of asian-americans and andean-americans in the United States have found homes throughout the metropolis.

People from all walks of life and incomes flood the sidewalks, but the city has become known as a bastion of political and social progression.

Homosexuality, in most areas, is celebrated, the homeless will interact with the wealthy, and protesters are common fixtures in major parks.

The Grid System

To Manhattanites, there are four basic directions: North, South, East, and West. NYC is one of the easiest cities to navigate (at least above 14th street) as its grid-formation holds no tricks.

In Manhattan, 'streets' run East to West, and 'avenues' run North to South. Thus, if you get out of a subway on 42nd Street and are trying to get to 40th Street, if you walk up one block and see 43rd Street, you know you need to turn around and walk the other way.

Avenues are spaced much further apart than Streets are, and there are only 11. The 12th Avenue is the West Side Highway along the Hudson River. The dividing line between East and West for most of Manhattan is 5th Avenue. Thus, if you see an address that reads 155 W 42nd Street, it will be number 155 West of 5th Avenue.

If you are walking some distance, it is fairly easy to estimate how long it will take you to walk. One block going north-south will take you about 1 minute to walk at a leisurely pace, one block going east-west will take you about 4 minutes.

As you make your way further downtown, past 1st Street on the East Side and past 14th Street on the West Side, the grid does disappear and the layout becomes more similar to many other world cities. The street layout here is more confusing, not as straight, and less familiar.

Outside of the island of Manhattan, such as in the boroughs, the grid system does not apply.

We recommend having a paper map with you, as well as a smartphone. This is because although cell phone reception is fine for most of Manhattan, you will find that the GPS regularly gets "confused" due to the large buildings and your location on your smartphone may not be accurate.

Internet Access

NYC has good cell phone coverage for data but this may be expensive for international visitors who may be best sticking to Wi-Fi hotspots when needing data.

Most hotels will include unlimited free Wi-Fi in the cost of your room. When out exploring the city, many restaurants also provide free Wi-Fi access for guests of the eating establishment.

McDonald's and Starbucks are the most common names for free Wi-Fi. If you happen to walk past an Apple Store, their Wi-Fi is free too.

Many public libraries also provide free Wi-Fi access – including the NY Public Library and the Mid-

Manhattan Library.

ATT Wireless and CableVision provide free Wi-Fi in New York City's parks, though these may have limits.

Making Phone Calls

You will want to make sure your mobile or cell phone works in the US. Modern smartphones will most likely work everywhere but some older phones, and non-smartphones, may be limited to your home country or region. Check before traveling.

You should be aware of roaming charges when visiting the US if you are an international visitor. Calls and text messages also often cost significantly more than they do back home. You may also be charged to receive calls and messages too. Data, in particular, can be extremely expensive so check with your network provider whether they offer roaming deals or packages.

Once in the US, you will need to dial an international code to make calls. For calls to the US, you should add 001 or +1 before the phone number you are calling.

Each area of the US has its own area code, for NYC's Manhattan area this is mainly 212. So, if you are dialling an NYC number from your cell phone, you would call 001212 or +1212, then the rest of the number.

If you need to make calls back to your own country when in the US, depending on how your network provider has set this up, you may need to enter your country's international dialling code, followed by the phone number. Other network providers may allow you to call your home country without the international code – this varies and is worth checking in advance.

Currency

The currency in use in New York City is the US Dollar. Checks (also known as "cheques") are not accepted in most places. As such, a mix of cash and credit is recommended. We recommend a pre-paid card or using a no-fee card from your home country.

For UK visitors, we recommend FairFx's pre-paid debit card. With our exclusive link you get the £9.95 card fee waived: http://bit.ly/debitdlp

Visa, Mastercard and American Express are the most widely accepted brands, with Maestro and Diners Club also accepted at select locations.

In the USA, unlike most countries, you may not always be asked for your PIN and may need to sign instead.

Contactless payments such as Apple Pay and Android Pay are accepted at some locations but are by no means universal. Contactless debit and credit cards are rare amongst American issued banks but your contactless card should work at most stores that take Apple Pay and Android Pay.

Know Before You Go

Weather

The coldest month is usually January. The average low is about 27 °F (-3 °C), but there will be regular drops to 10 °F (-12 °C) for days and sometimes weeks at a time. Snowfall varies, but in recent years January and February have yielded significant amounts of snow, often over 50 centimeters (20 inches).

Although summer temperatures lie at a sensible average 82 °F (28 °C), it can feel warmer as humidity levels are high and industrial systems (such as the subway, restaurants, etc.) constantly emit heat that gets trapped in the streets.

Spring and fall (autumn) are often unpredictable and fleeting. Temperatures in NYC usually fall within a range, but it is not uncommon for them to be erratic. April, May, September, and October are generally considered the mildest months.

Rainfall is relatively consistent throughout the year, with monthly rainfall averaging between 3 and 4 inches. Each month has 10 to 15 rainy days on average, with Spring being the wettest season. February experiences the least rain but even this is only a marginal difference.

Month by Month Temperature Averages:

Month	Low (C/F)	High (C/F)	Month	Low (C/F)	High (C/F)
January	-3/27	6/43	July	20/67	29/84
February	-3/27	7/44	August	20/67	28/82
March	1/35	9/48	September	16/60	24/75
April	6/42	16/61	October	10/50	18/64
May	12/54	20/68	November	5/41	12/54
June	17/62	27/80	December	4/40	12/54

Typical NYC Food

When it comes to food and drink, there is nothing NYC doesn't have. Any craving can be satisfied, and often within a five-block radius. While quality does vary, New York's food standard is, by and large, pretty high.

Be sure to try the NYC staples. NYC is famed for its bagels, pizza, hot dogs, cheesecake, and other delights. New Yorkers will debate for hours about the best place to get a bagel or a slice of pizza. While you will find examples in the neighborhood guides in this book, here are the best of the New York classics.

Bagels:
• Absolute Bagels – 2788 Broadway
• Ess-a-Bagel – 831 3rd Avenue
• Brooklyn Bagel & Coffee Company – 286 8th Avenue

Pizza Slices:
• Famous Joe's Pizza – 7 Carmine Street
• Sal and Carmine – 2671 Broadway
• Grimaldi's – 656 6th Avenue & 1 Front Street, Brooklyn

Cheesecake:
• Junior's – 386 Flatbush Avenue, Brooklyn
• Eileen's Special Cheesecake – 17 Cleveland Place
• Lady M Confections – 41 E 78th Street

Hot Dogs:
• Nathan's Famous – 1310 Surf Avenue, Brooklyn
• Gray's Papaya – 2090 Broadway (other locations)
• Dirty Water Hot Dogs – Sold on street corner pushcarts around NYC

NYC Customs and Etiquette

Walking
New Yorkers tend to walk quickly, whether they are in a rush or not, and they do not like to slow down their cadence. If you are in a big group, avoiding taking up the entire sidewalk. Always leave a path around you.

Stopping abruptly on a sidewalk is also fairly taboo. It is wise to take a quick look over your shoulder, and stop on one side of the sidewalk as you would when driving.

Elevator Etiquette
This is very important to New Yorkers. At hotels, museums, or places where there are many tourists, this does not apply. However, in offices and residential buildings, there are a couple of rules to consider.

Remember, many buildings in NYC have more than 10 stories. So, if everyone gets into an elevator and presses their individual floors, it can take 4 to 5 minutes for the people who live or work up at the top to get off.

If you are a healthy adult, it is customary to skip the elevator and walk if you have less than 3 floors to go up or down.

Also, as the floor numbers get bigger you should consider whether you need to press your floor's button at all. If you are within a flight or two of a number that has already been pressed, the expectation is that you will normally get out and take a flight down or up. For example, if you are going to the 22nd floor, and you get on an elevator and number 23 has already been pressed, you are expected to get off on the 23rd floor and take the stairs down. If you are disabled, on crutches, or elderly, this does not apply.

Smoking
Since 2003, a state law has restricted where people can and cannot smoke. It is illegal to smoke in all enclosed spaces, with a few exceptions including cigar bars, private homes and tobacco businesses. It is also not allowed on public transportation, including all buses and subways. Smoking is also forbidden in parks, beaches, pedestrian plazas (like Times Square), swimming pools, and select other locations.

Electronic cigarettes are subject to the same restrictions as regular cigarettes. The minimum age to buy tobacco, cigarettes and e-cigarettes in NYC is 21.

Tipping
Tipping in NYC is essentially, although not legally, mandatory. Tips pay the majority of many employees' paychecks.

Waiters and waitresses make tiny salaries and rely on tips to live. Even at high-end restaurants, many staff live in the outer boroughs; many people in the hospitality industry in NYC are pursuing other careers and dreams, and are keeping a job to support themselves.

Tipping 15 to 20% of the check before taxes is standard. Most New Yorkers tip on the higher end: at least 18%. Tips of 15% are increasingly rare.

Often with bigger groups – over five or six people – the tip is automatically added, so be careful and read the check every time. Many card machines will propose a minimum tip of 20%, but you can change this.

Tipping doesn't just stop at wait staff, however. Bartenders will expect $1 per round, bell hops get $1 per bag (more if they are heavy), tour guides are commonly tipped 10% to 15% of the tour price, and for taxi drivers its about 15%. If you ask your hotel's concierge service for help, a tip of $1 to $2 is fair for calling you a cab, and $3 to $5 for a restaurant or show reservation – more if these are hard to secure. Be sure to have quite a few $1 bills on you for tips.

Payment in restaurants may seem odd to international visitors. On the check for your meal, you will have the total price and an area asking how much you would like to tip. Your card is then swiped for payment for the total amount – initially only the meal price is deducted, later this is adjusted to include the tip.

Chapter Three | Getting to NYC

Getting to NYC

Before you explore the 'Big Apple', you first need to get there. For the majority of visitors from around the world this will mean flying in to one of New York City's airports. However, this is far from the only option: driving, trains and long-distance buses are other ways to reach the city.

Flying

The airports that most people fly into are: LaGuardia Airport, John F. Kennedy (JFK) International Airport, and Newark Liberty International Airport just over the bridge in New Jersey.

LaGuardia is primarily a domestic airport while JFK and Newark serve more international flights.

LaGuardia Airport

Mainly used for flights within the US, La Guardia Airport is in the process of being renovated in phases to modernize it. It is the least busy of the three NYC airports.

A bus, the NYC Airporter, runs every 30 minutes to midtown Manhattan – Port Authority, Grand Central Station, and Penn Station. Tickets are $16 one way ($30 roundtrip) and can be purchased online at www.NYCAirporter.com.

Other public transit options are the MTA public buses.

The M60 goes to upper Manhattan through Queens and the Q70 takes you to Midtown Manhattan near a lot of subway stops. The bus fare is $2.75 with a MetroCard or you can purchase a $3.00 single ride ticket. There is no direct subway link to or from the airport.

Taxis are available and you should only use certified Yellow Taxis. There are often black cars, known as gypsy cabs, which are illegal and may charge much higher rates. From LaGuardia to Manhattan the fares will be anywhere between $30 and $40. The taxis are metered which means the more traffic, the more expensive it will be.

Uber and Lyft are also options. Use our exclusive link at www.uber.com/invite/uberindependentguides for $15 in free Uber credit.

Car rentals are also available but few people choose to drive in NYC. It is mainly a hassle and parking is often very expensive and cumbersome.

10 The Independent Guide to New York City

Newark Liberty Airport

Newark is the second biggest airport serving New York City and handles both domestic and international flights.

From Newark, there are several transportation options to reach the city.

The Air Train connects to NJ Transit or Amtrak (NJ Transit is cheaper), which will take you to Manhattan's Penn Station. This is the cheaper, and often quickest option - about 30 minutes total. It will cost you $12.50.

There are also a number of private shuttle bus offerings from Newark to Manhattan that range from $15 to $60 each way. Companies include Go Airlink NYC, Newark Liberty Airport Express, Super Shuttle and NYC Airporter.

A taxi from Newark to Manhattan will run you somewhere between $50 to $70, not including tolls. This is a metered fare. Uber is also available is likely to be cheaper than a yellow cab.

J.F.K. International Airport

J.F.K. International Airport is by far the largest of the city's airports. It has good transportation links and is particularly popular for its links with Europe.

There are a number of public transportation options to get to and from JFK. Most people take the AirTrain, which drops off at Jamaica Station - here NYC buses and three subway lines run to the rest of Manhattan.

The Airtrain also goes to Howard Beach Station where the A train and the Q11 bus run. The whole trip from the airport to Manhattan using the Airtrain and subway takes about 1 hour (10 minutes on the AirTrain itself) and costs $7.75 (including a transfer to the subway or bus).

The NYC Airporter bus is another option and departs every 30 minutes, costing $18-$19 one way, or $35 roundtrip.

If you want to take a taxi, JFK offers a flat fare of $52, plus tolls and tip to anywhere in Manhattan. There is a $4.50 surcharge from 4:00pm to 8:00pm on weekdays.

Uber and Lyft also operate from the airport but may be more expensive than cabs as they may not offer a flat rate.

Rail Services

If you are travelling domestically, taking a train to NYC can be a great idea. New York Penn Station is conveniently located in Midtown West where you can easily find public transportation to anywhere in Manhattan. Amtrak, LIRR, and NJ Transit lines all run through Penn Station. Grand Central Terminal is another hub, mostly used by commuters. The lines run north to upstate New York and Connecticut.

Bus Services

Buses are often the cheapest way of travelling domestically. Many go back and forth between the Port Authority, such as Greyhound, MegaBus, and Bolt buses. There are also buses that run more local routes (e.g. Boston or Washington D.C.) that are very inexpensive and depart from Chinatown. Booking these in advance is important as they can often be full.

Chapter Four | Transportation in NYC

Transportation in NYC

Transportation in NYC is abundant and extremely important in getting around. You will rarely have to wait more than five minutes for either a subway, a bus or a taxi during normal hours.

Subway

The subway is the preferred method of getting around the city for many. It runs 24 hours a day, with limited service late in the evenings and on weekends - not all lines operate between midnight and 6:00am.

Although the same did not hold true in the 1970s, the subways now are relatively safe. During weekdays in Manhattan they remain populated until about midnight. Also, many plain clothed and uniformed policemen are in and around the system.

That said, keeping an eye on your belongings in crowded subway 'cars' (the New York term for subway carriages) is always a good idea. It is smart to put your bag between your legs or on your stomach as pick pockets do operate – always keep your belongings in front of you, particularly at rush hour.

The subway is structured by number/letter and color. This is both simple and complicated. Within Manhattan, most trains of the same color run on the same line, however, one or two of them will run express routes.

Express route trains do not stop at all stations. This is important to know, because

if you simply get on a train of the right color, it may not stop where you want to get off.

The good news is that every time you enter the subway system, you have as many free rides and transfers until you exit. Thus, if you do make a mistake, simply get off at the next stop, take the stairs to the opposite platform, and go in the other direction. However, it is important to keep an eye out for the Local/Express trains and understand how to properly read the map.

Before entering through the ticket barriers, be sure to know whether you want to go generally North (Uptown) or South (Downtown). This is because many local stops (and some express stops) have one entrance on one side of the street for Uptown trains and another entrance on

the other side of the street for Downtown trains. If the station entrance is Uptown or Downtown only, this will be clearly marked at the entrance to the station (like in the photo below).

If traveling at night, do look out for the orb-lamposts outside subway stations - green means the entrance is open 24/7, and red means that entrance closes at night. Some orbs will be fully green or red, and others will be red or green on top and white at the bottom - these are merely aesthetic differences and they mean the same.

12 The Independent Guide to New York City

Understanding the Subway Map:

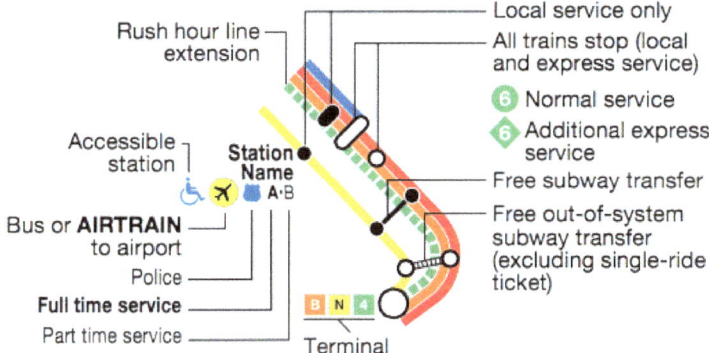

On the subway map, you will see all of the stops and the lines, which are clearly indicated by their colors.

On the map, black dots indicate that there is a stop, but only local trains stop there. White dots indicate that both local and express service trains stop there. If a white or black dot covers multiple lines on the map, a transfer between those lines is available.

A black line connecting two small dots means a transfer available, but it usually requires a longer walk through an underground passageway.

Express Trains and Local Trains:

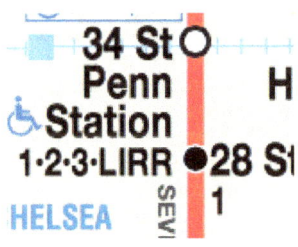

Next to each stop number, you will see a small number or letter combination – this indicates which of the colored trains stop at a given station.

For example, on the 1/2/3 line, next to Penn Station it shows that all three trains stop there. However, at 28th street, only the 1 is listed. This is because the 1 is local and the 2 and 3 are express trains.

Here are the express/local trains for each line:
- A/C/E: C – Local; A/E – Express
- 1/2/3: 1 – Local; 2/3 – Express
- 4/5/6: 6 – Local; 4/5 – Express
- N/Q/R: R – Local; Q/N – Express
- B/D/F/M: M – Local; BDF - Express

Pricing:

Subway fares in New York are a flat rate no matter how far you travel and for a major city are relatively affordable. They are cheaper than London's fares, for example, but more expensive than Paris'.

Subway fares are loaded onto thin, plastic MetroCards, which can be used both on subways and local buses. A metro card costs $1 and you can then add subway rides to it, or cash. If you are on a budget it is important to be economical. Here is the breakdown of pricing:

• **Pay-Per Ride**
- Buy as many rides as you want
- A single MetroCard ride costs $2.75
- Load up to $80 on the card at a time. A 5% bonus credit is added to your card when you load at least $5.50 in one transaction.

• **Single Ride ticket**
- $3.00 for one ride. No transfers. Valid for 2 hours.

•**7-Day Unlimited**
- $32.00
- Unlimited subway and local bus rides until midnight.

• **30-Day Unlimited**
- $121
- Unlimited subway and local bus rides for 30 days.

•**7-Day Express Bus Plus**
- $59.50
- Unlimited express bus, local bus, and subway rides for 7 days. It is unlikely you will need express buses as a visitor.

Important to note:
• If you are planning on fewer than 13 rides in a week or 47 rides in a month, then the Pay-Per-Ride rates (with the 5% bonus) are the best value for you. Otherwise, you should either get a 7-Day Unlimited or 30-Day Unlimited card.
• Up to three children, 44 inches tall and under, ride for free when accompanied by a fare-paying adult on subways and local buses.
• Infants (under two years of age) ride express buses free if the child sits on the lap of the accompanying adult.
• On unlimited cards, there is a time limit that goes into effect after one swipe. Thus, you cannot buy an unlimited card for two people, and swipe one person right after the other. A grace period of about 20 minutes goes into effect after one swipe to ensure that everyone has his or her own card.
• Not all stations have people working to help you. There are automated machines where you can purchase tickets. These are usually reliable.
• The direction you are going will be indicated by a sign that usually says "Downtown" or "Uptown" or the last name of the stop of that line.
• Upon exiting, there are usually multiple stairwells that lead to corners dictated by North/South/East/West. If you are meeting someone, ask them which exit to use to save yourself walking all the way around the block.

Top Tip: If you are using Pay Per Ride, up to four people can share the same card. Simply swipe the MetroCard for the number of people riding and then walk through the turnstile consecutively. Alternatively, each person can swipe and walk through and then pass the card back.

Buses

While buses in NYC are available, most people prefer the subway in Manhattan due to the traffic. Subways run primarily up and down town, while buses frequently run across town.

The fares are the same as they are for the subway, and you can transfer at certain locations without paying an extra fee. The exception to this is the express buses for long-distance trips – here the fare is not $2.75 per ride, but $6.50.

If you are planning on using the buses, Google Maps is a helpful resource for journey planning.

Cycling

Cycling as a form of transportation in NYC has become increased immensely in popularity in recent years. Bike lanes are available on many streets and they are well used. For the most part in downtown and mid-town, the roads in Manhattan are flat, with no hills.

It is perfectly acceptable to tour NYC by bike but you should be advised that cab drivers, NYC cyclists, and pedestrians, operate at their own pace and it can be a threatening place to ride.

Make sure you are going the right way on one-way streets, stay in the bike lanes if they are available, and be vigilant about your surroundings.

There are a number of bike rental options throughout the city and there is the option to use the Citi Bike program. You can get 24 hours of rides for unlimited 30-minute trips for $12 or 3 days of rides for $24. A single 30-minute ride is $3. Trips over 30 minutes in length cost extra.

Although the Citi Bike program allows flexibility, most visitors to the city will still choose to use the subway as it is far less tiring.

Cabs

There is always the option of grabbing a cab in NYC. You will see them everywhere.

All cabs have lights on the top. If the light is on, there is a vacancy. If the light is off, the cab is not available for hire. To hail a cab, you simply wave them over. They will pull to the side of the street and when you hop in they will ask for your destination.

Taxi rides are metered and both time and distance affect the rate. If there is a lot of traffic, rates will be higher. Cabs are technically not allowed to turn you down but late at night, or at the end of long shifts, many will reject rides if they are not in the direction of the cab driver's home.

The base rate of a cab fare is $2.50 plus 50 cents per 1/5 of a mile, or 50 cents per 1 minute in slow traffic or when the vehicle is stopped. Passengers pay all tolls and surcharges.

A surcharge of at least $0.80 is added to each fare, and there may be a peak time surcharge of $1 too depending on when you travel. There is no charge for extra passengers or luggage.

NYC cabs take cash and cards for all amounts, but individual bills over $20 are generally not accepted. A tip of at least 15% will be expected in addition to the fare shown on the meter.

Be careful of gypsy or illegal cabs. These are black cars that will pull over when you are trying to hail taxis and may try and charge you a flat

rate. These cars are illegal and may overcharge you. It is better to stay with the yellow cab service.

Other popular (and usually cheaper) options are Uber and Lyft - these run with smartphone applications. You connect your credit card to the application and the payment processes automatically. Get $15 of free credit for Uber by using our exclusive link at www.uber.com/invite/uberindependentguides.

Top 10 Must-See Attractions

❶ Metropolitan Museum of Art
Known locally as The Met, this museum is the largest art museum in the United States and has been in operation since 1872. There are 17 curatorial departments and the permanent collection has over two million works from all over the world.

The outside architecture alone is worth seeing. The walls, stairs and columns are influenced by Beaux-Arts architecture of neoclassical style.

❷ Times Square
Times Square is a tourist's mecca; it is a commercial intersection that goes from West 42nd to West 47th Street and convenes at Broadway.

It is Times Square that has given NYC the reputation as the 'City of Light', and it is certainly a must-see on any itinerary.

The area is also known as the Theater District, as the surrounding streets house many of the city's musicals and plays.

❸ Central Park
Central Park is a bit of an enigma; it is the antithesis of Manhattan, yet it blends so seamlessly into the island that it would be impossible to imagine the city today without it.

It is a reminder to its residents of the nature and serenity that exists in so much of the world that is so rarely seen in this city. As the weather gets nice in the city, New Yorkers flock to the grassy fields in droves.

❹ The High Line
The High Line is a relatively new addition to NYC, added in 2009. This linear park was built on an elevated section of a railroad called the West Side Line. It extends from Gansevoort Street to 34th Street and is best experienced by walking its length.

It passes under the Chelsea Market – a sizable food hall on 15th Street – where many visitors break for a meal, and it is situated over the various art galleries that Chelsea is famed for

❺ MoMA
The Museum of Modern Art (MoMA) is renowned for housing some of the most important modern art in the world.

Though it has been in operation since the early 1900s, renovations in 1983 and 2002 have doubled its original gallery size and have made the place an open and modern structure.

The permanent collections are considered some of the best in world with famous artists including Salvador Dali, Claude Monet, Henri Matisse, Andy Warhol, Pablo Picasso and Vincent Van Gogh.

Top 10 Attractions

6 Brooklyn Bridge
The Brooklyn Bridge is a unique fixture not just in New York, but also in the world. The hybrid cable-stayed/suspension bridge was completed in 1883 and it connects lower Manhattan to Dumbo and Brooklyn Heights.

The length of the bridge is 1.1 miles (and 1.8 kilometers) long. There is no charge to access the bridge.

7 Tenement Museum
The Tenement Museum is an unassuming institution on the Lower East Side that successfully brings the history of immigrants living in NYC between 1869 and 1935 to life.

For those interested in history, this is a prime spot to go, and for those not so interested, this is the place that may spark your curiosity.

The museum is only seen through guided tours.

8 9/11 Memorial
The events of September 11, 2001 greatly changed NYC, and its residents have not forgotten them. In 2011, this memorial opened. Michael Arad and Peter Walker's design, "Reflecting Absence" was chosen and construction began in 2006.

The memorial consists of two one-acre pools with the largest man-made waterfalls in the United States. The victims' names are inscribed on bronze plates that are attached to the walls of the pools. Trees fill the rest of the 6 acres of the plaza. The memorial is respectful, peaceful and breathtaking.

9 Top of The Rock
Although the Empire State Building has views of the city, the experience of going to the Top of Rockefeller Plaza yields the best views of anywhere in the NYC area, in our opinion.

At the top is an indoor space with comfortable seating and floor-to-ceiling windows where you can enjoy remarkable views. An outdoor space is also available on several levels.

10 The Cloisters
Located in the northern tip of Manhattan in Fort Tyron Park in the neighborhood of Washington Heights, this is an extension of The Met. The museum exhibits art, architecture, and artifacts from Medieval Europe.

What makes it such a unique place is the setting; it is situated on top of a hill, which overlooks the Hudson River. The landscaping was done in a curatorial way with horticultural information used from medieval archives to create a representative botanical experience.

Chapter Six | Neighborhood Guides

Neighborhood Guides

Now it's time to take a look at New York City by taking a look at each neighborhood individually. New York City is more than just Manhattan, so this section covers the main island as well as all outer boroughs.

As we look through each neighborhood, we have included a brief description and history of the area, a look at accommodation options, along with popular hotspots and places to eat. Organizing the guide in this manner allows you to find a neighborhood you like, and then find local places to stay and dine.

In this section, where subway transportation is listed, we state the train number/letter followed by where you should get off. E.g. "1 to 125th Street" means you should take the '1' train to the '125th Street' stop.

Each attraction, restaurant and accommodation listed features a fact sheet with symbols, the key below helps to explain what each of these symbols means.

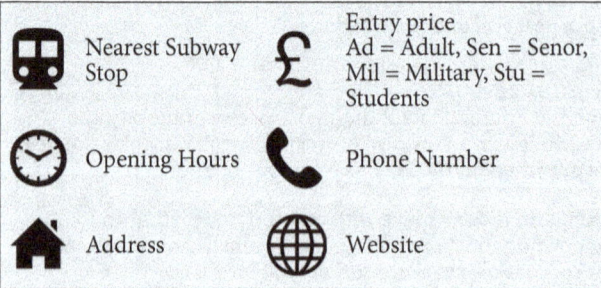

🚇	Nearest Subway Stop	£	Entry price Ad = Adult, Sen = Senor, Mil = Military, Stu = Students
🕐	Opening Hours	📞	Phone Number
🏠	Address	🌐	Website

Neighborhood Guide: Harlem

Harlem

Harlem is most often associated with the Harlem Renaissance – an era during the 1920s and 1930s in the United States when African-American cultural expression flourished and rose to prominence. While the neighborhood has certainly changed, it holds onto its history and identity as one of the most progressive black neighborhoods in the United States by preserving some of the establishments and practices that brought it critical acclaim.

After World War II and the Great Depression, Harlem saw a significant economic downfall. Race riots and protests, ultimately contributed to the Civil Rights movement in the United States, and Harlem became known as a poor and dangerous neighborhood.

Since the 2000s many renovations have taken place and the neighborhood is growing economically again, and changing at a fast rate.

As far as safety is concerned this is still a touchy subject. Although many people feel perfectly safe in Harlem,

this is a very large area and therefore there are all kinds of different people and safety varies. There are still some very rough parts of the area, particularly around the housing projects along 8th Avenue and between 130th and 145th Streets.

On the other hand, there are very many churchgoers in Harlem too, and the area contains some of the city's most beautiful architecture.

The most frequented parts of Harlem by tourists are based around 125th Street. Use your common sense as you walk around, as you would anywhere else in the city.

See and Do

El Museo del Barrio

	4/6 to 103rd Street		elmuseo.org
	Wed to Sat 11:00am to 6:00pm, Sun midday to 5:00pm		1230 Fifth Avenue
	Adults: $9, Students & seniors: $5; Unders 12: Free. Free for all every 3rd Sat of the month.		

Often referred to as simply, "El Museo," this museum has transformed from a Fire Station to a space that stores 8,500 pieces of pre-Columbian works and artifacts, as well as contemporary art.

The inspiration came about during the Nuyorican Movement – a cultural movement during the Civil Rights Era when Puerto Ricans living in NYC began to demand equal rights and treatment.

A partnership with the Museum of the City of New York allows you to visit both museums for the admission price of one.

Cotton Club

 1 to 125th Street

 Swing dance: $25; Dinner: $56.50; Fridays night: $20 cover; Gospel show: $43.50

 See description

 cottonclub-newyork.com

 656 W 125th Street

From 1923 to 1935, the Cotton Club was NYC's premier nightclub. Although it was a whites-only venue, many black performers – including Louis Armstrong, Ethel Waters and Billie Holiday – performed here.

The club closed in 1936 as a result of race riots and boycotts surrounding the racial prejudice. It reopened later that year in Midtown until 1940 when it proved too expensive to run.

In the 1970s they built a replica of the original, which still stands today.

Schedule: Swing dance Mon from 8:00pm; Dinner Thurs from 8:00pm & Sat from 9:00pm; Jazz & Blues on Fridays; Gospel show weekends 12:00 & 14:30.

Apollo Theater

 A/B/C/D to 125th Street; 2/3 to 125th Street

 apollotheater.org

 Tours: Mon, Tues, Thur, & Fri at 11:00am, 1:00pm & 3:00pm; Wed at 11:00am; Weekends at 11:00am & 1:00pm

 253 W 125th Street

 Prices vary per show

The Apollo was originally a Burlesque Theater in 1913 to 1914 as a whites-only venue.

In 1934, Sidney Cohen reopened the venue, with the hope of catering to black musical artists and audience members.

Notable artists that performed there include Duke Ellington, Sam Cooke, Aretha Franklin, Otis Redding and Ray Charles.

After the 1960s the theater saw a decline, and after a few different owners, it was purchased by the State of New York. It is now registered as a NYC Landmark and draws 1.3 million visitors a year.

Historic tours last one hour and are offered 2 to 3 times daily, except Wednesdays when they offer a special package with tickets for the Amateur Night. Tour tickets must be purchased in advance and cost $17 per person on weekdays and $19 on weekends. Performances take place regularly.

Neighborhood Guide: Harlem

Schomburg Center for Research in Black Culture

 2/3 to 135th Street

 nypl.org/locations/schomburg

 Mon, Thurs & Fri 10:00am to 6:00pm; Tues and Wed 10:00am to 8:00pm. Closed on weekends.

 515 Malcolm X Boulevard

 Free entry

Although a Library may not be the first place you want to visit, the Schomburg Center for Research in Black Culture is unique and historically significant.

The Library opened in 1905 after Andrew Carnegie funded the building of 65 branch libraries throughout the city. In the 1920s, black people were integrated into the staff and they held the first exhibition of African-American art in Harlem.

African-American scholar Arturo Alfonso Schomburg donated and sold his enormous collection to be made available to the public in 1926. In 1942 an extension was built.

In 1980 the new Schomburg Center was founded, and the original building on 135th street was named a NYC Landmark. Since 1998 it has been considered the best Afrocentric artifact collection of any public library in the United States.

The Center has five divisions – Art and Artifacts, Research and References, Manuscripts and Archives and Rare Books, Moving Image and Recorded Sound, and Photographs and Prints. There are also readings, art exhibitions and theatrical events open to the public.

Eat

Abyssinia Restaurant
Open: *Daily midday to 10:00pm*
Address: *268 W 135th Street*
Telephone: *212-281-2673*
Website: *harlemethiopianfood.com*
Subway: *A/B/C to 135th Street; 2/3 to 135th Street*

The owners of Abyssinia were Ethiopians that began selling Injera in bulk from their apartment 8 years ago – a rarity in NYC. They originally only sold products to Ethiopians. Now they have a restaurant that serves up authentic Ethiopian fare to everyone.

With a large and growing Ethiopian population throughout the city, the reception has been positive.

The vegetable dishes, and meat and lentil stews, run from $12 to $15 per entrée, or you can get a combination platter and try them all. They also serve honey wine.

Red Rooster
Open: *Mon to Fri 11:30am to 3:30pm & 4:30pm to 10:30pm; Sat 10:00am to 3:00pm & 4:30pm to 11:30pm; Sun 10:00am to 3:00pm & 4:30am to 10:00pm*
Address: *310 Lenox Avenue*
Telephone: *212-792-9001*
Website: *redroosterharlem.com*
Subway: *2/3 to 125th Street; A/C/B/D to 125th Street*

Named after a legendary Speakeasy in Harlem during the Prohibition Era, Andrew Chapman and Marcus Samuelsson opened this restaurant to celebrate Harlem's history and vibrant culture.

Samuelsson is an award-winning chef, cookbook author, and the youngest chef to receive two three-star ratings from the New York Times.

The menu boasts interesting adaptations to southern classics, as well as the dishes in their original form. Dishes like Macaroni and Cheese and Collard Greens ($9) and Barbeque Pork Ribs ($29) embody some of the classic entrées. However, Ethiopian inspired dishes can also be found amidst the menu.

A brunch menu is also available, as well as an eclectic cocktail menu. Sometimes the restaurant doubles as an art space.

Dinosaur Bar-B-Que
Open: *Mon to Thurs 11:30am to 11:00pm; Fri & Sat 11:30am to 12:00am; Sun 12:00pm to 10:00pm*
Address: *700 W 125th Street*
Telephone: *212-694-1777*
Website: *dinosaurbarbque.com*
Subway: *1 to 125th Street*

The concept and execution of this nationally acclaimed Bar-B-Que chain began in upstate New York during the 1980s by some motorcyclists. Throughout the 1990s and early 2000s, they have opened eight locations.

They've been named the country's best BBQ on Good Morning America and the chain is highly regarded by other commercial publications. The atmosphere is fun and lively. There is often a considerable wait, but most people think it's worth it.

Their famed homemade BBQ sauce can even be bought separately.

Many are fans of their Brisket and Pulled Pork Plates ($18 and $17) as well as their Creole Spiced Deviled Eggs ($4/$7/$13). Sandwiches will run you about $12 while plates are more in the range of $18-$25. Servings are big and can certainly be shared. They even have a Vegetarian Smoke Portobello ($12) and gluten free options are available so everyone can find something. Finally, they have over 25 beers on tap.

Stay

Aloft Harlem
Address: *2296 Frederick Douglass Boulevard*
Telephone: *212-749-4000*
Website: *aloftharlem.com*
Subway: *A/B/C/D to 125th Street; 2/3 to 125th Street*

Aloft Harlem is a newly renovated hotel with modern design and loft-inspired rooms. There is a bar, a pool table, free Wi-Fi, and free bottles of water for guests.

Many families visiting Columbia University opt to stay here, as it is just a short 10-minute walk away.

Most regard it as nothing all too special, but good value for the money. Rooms are usually between $240 to $270 per night.

The International Cozy Inn
Address: *248 Malcolm X Blvd*
Telephone: *646-248-1890*
Website: *theinternationalcozyinn.com*
Subway: *2/3 to 125th Street*

This hotel is a very quirky and unique option that is great for travelling with the family or a few friends.

There are different suite-style options available, each decorated with bright patterned betting, and some with kitchens and closed fireplaces.

If you're staying in NYC for a longer period of time and don't mind falling asleep to bright colors and somewhat unmatchable décor, this is a great option.

Prices range from $50 to $80 per person for a 4-person minimum suite, and move up from there.

Harlem YMCA
Address: *180 West 135th Street*
Telephone: *212-912-2100*
Website: *ymcanyc.org/association/guest-rooms/harlemrooms*
Subway: *2/3 to 135th Street; B/C to 135th Street*

For those travelling on a strict budget, the Harlem YMCA is a good option for lodging. With complimentary luggage storage, a breakfast voucher, free Wi-Fi, and no curfew, this is an ideal place for young people who are constantly exploring. Additionally, a pool and gym are available for use. Rooms start from $100/night for a single room or $70 if shared.

Neighborhood Guide: Upper West Side

Upper West Side

Located close to Columbia University, the Upper West Side is a residential area for the upwardly mobile cultural and intellectual crowd. Until the turn of the 20th century, the area was largely considered the countryside, as it had not been developed yet. However, with the development of the rail lines and public transportation, people began to settle in upper Manhattan.

The first residents of the Upper West Side were largely African-Americans, many of whom were veterans of the Spanish-American War. Many scenes in the musical 'West Side Story' were filmed among the tenement streets, highlighting racial and gang tensions in the area.

After World War II, a combination of gay white men and young college graduates began populating the Upper West Side, gentrifying the neighborhood. Tenements were torn down and the now-multimillion dollar brownstones were built, as were a series of gigantic modern apartment buildings owned by Donald Trump looking out on the Hudson River.

The area now is much whiter and more affluent, but minority populations still exist. It's a pleasant place to walk around – the sidewalks are wide, quiet, and you are rarely more than a short walk from Central Park.

See and Do

New York Historical Society

 A/B/C to 81st Street

 nyhistory.org

 Tues to Thurs and Sat 10:00am to 6:00pm; Fri 10:00am to 8:00pm; Sun 11:00am to 5:00pm. Closed Mon.

 170 Central Park West

 Adults: $21, Seniors & military: $16, Students: $13, Ages 5-13: $6, Under 5: Free

In 1804, the New York Historical Society became New York's first museum. It has been at the current location since 1908, and is an excellent place for those interested in American history.

The institution is known for unique innovations, such as a two-year exhibit held about slavery in New York, which began in 2005.

The exhibitions cover many topics throughout American history, but they are always well-researched and put together comprehensively.

It has over 1.6 million works in its permanent collections and has maintained its prestige as a premiere research institution. There is also a separate Children's Museum, with interactive exhibits and a theater.

Pay-as-you-wish from 6:00pm to 8:00pm on Fridays.

American Museum of Natural History

 A/B/C to 81st Street

 Ad: $23, Stu and sen: $18, Children (2 to 12): $13

 Daily 10:00am to 5:45pm

 amnh.org

 Central Park West at 79th Street

Often seen on signs and pamphlets as AMNH, the American Museum of Natural History comprises 27 interconnected buildings, as well as a planetarium and library.

With over 32 million specimens scattered throughout the 1.6 million square feet space, this is one of the largest museums in the world and makes for a fascinating visit.

The exhibits are interesting for both adults and children alike with many interactive sections.

There are additional ticketed events, such as 2D and 3D film showings, as well as special exhibitions and limited-time offerings.

Beacon Theatre

 1/2/3 to 72nd Street

 212-465-6500

 beacontheatre.com

 2124 Broadway

The Beacon Theatre was initially a deluxe movie palace for films and vaudeville. It opened in 1929 but was bought out in 1974 to become a music venue. It has hosted countless famous artists such as the Grateful Dead and the Allman Brothers Band.

The neo-Grecian architecture makes it a place to marvel at while walking to your seat.

Renovations in 2009 revamped the venue while maintaining its authentic appeal. Big music artists and groups perform here on a regular basis and it is truly a sight to be seen.

Neighborhood Guide: Upper West Side

American Folk Art Museum

 1 to 66th Street

 folkartmuseum.org

 Tues to Thur 11:30am to 7:00pm; Fri 12:00pm to 7:30pm; Sat 11:30 to 7:00pm; Sun 12:00 to 6:00pm. Closed Mon.

 2 Lincoln Square

 Free

This museum praises self-taught artists and folk artists from the around the United States. Since 1961, the museum has continuously grown and experienced a rise in acclaim.

It has over 5,000 objects from the 18th century and 7,000 items of the entire collection have been given as gifts. The temporary exhibitions usually focus on the self-taught artists, which results in unique and innovative visual pieces of work.

Lincoln Center

 1 to 66th Street

 lc.lincolncenter.org

 Tours daily between 10:30am and 4:00pm

 10 Lincoln Center Plaza

 Ad: $25, Students and Seniors: $20

Lincoln Center is a well-renowned complex with various facilities relating to the performance arts.

Some of the most notable performance spaces include Avery Fisher Hall, home to the New York Philharmonic, the Metropolitan Opera House, home to the Metropolitan Opera, the Julliard School, and Jazz at Lincoln Center, a premier jazz venue.

The entire institution is the world's largest presenter of performing arts and offers over 5,000 programs throughout the year.

Numerous events are offered daily.

Prices quoted above are for tours.

Eat

Alice's Tea Cup
Open: *Daily 8:00am to 8:00pm*
Address: *102 West 73rd Street*
Telephone: *518-889-9344*
Website: *alicesteacup.com*
Subway: *1/2/3 to 72nd Street; B/C to 72nd Street*

This shop, self-dubbed "New York City's most whimsical tea house!" plays off of the novel and movie, *Alice in Wonderland*, in every way.

With three locations throughout the city, they have mastered the art of scone baking and tea making, and have expanded the menu to other meals.

Whether you want a simple scone and tea (including a vegan one) or a decadent meal, this place will satisfy all cravings. Their extensive breakfast menu includes things like Wonderland Waffles ($12) or Alice's Florentine – Sautéed spinach and poached eggs on top of a buttermilk scone ($15).

They also offer a range of sandwiches and salads, but most people come for the baked goods.

Absolute Bagels
Open: *Daily 6:00am to 9:00pm.*
Address: *2788 Broadway*
Telephone: *212-932-2052*
Subway: *1 to Cathedral Pkwy*

As most New Yorkers will know, a cheap unassuming awning atop a storefront that serves bagels is generally a good sign. This old tradition is a sacred one in NYC, and a modernized atmosphere is seldom seen in correspondence with the quality. In NYC, Absolute Bagels is one of the best.

There is often a line wrapped around the corner, so get there before your hunger sets. On Saturday and Sunday mornings it can be especially crowded. The line moves quickly and there are a wide range of both bagels and toppings (including various cream cheeses) to choose from ($3 to $8).

There is very limited seating but Riverside Park is just a five-minute walk towards the river and is the perfect place for a picnic on a nice day.

Boulud Sud
Open: *Lunch: Mon to Fri 11:30am to 2:30pm, Dinner: Mon 5:00pm to 10:30pm, Tue to Sat 5:00pm to 11:30pm, Sun 5:00pm to 10:00pm, Brunch weekends 11:00am to 3:00pm*
Address: *20 West 64th Street*
Telephone: *212-595-1313*
Website: *bouludsud.com*
Subway: *1/2 to 66th Street*

For those seeking a fine dining experience Boulud Sud is a good option. Famous Chef Boulud's menu features Mediterranean-inspired dishes with an emphasis on grilled fish, lamb, and fresh vegetables.

The lunch menu features items like Kale and Harissa Shakshoula, with potatoes, goat cheese, and a soft-cooked hen egg ($22) as well as Za'atar grilled Mediterranean Sea Bass ($36). The restaurant also offers a pre-theater prix fixe menu served from 5:00pm to 7:00pm, Monday to Saturday. For $65, you can get an appetizer, entrée, and dessert.

Gennaro
Open: *Sun to Thurs 5:00pm to 10:30pm; Fri & Sat 5:00pm to 11:00pm*
Address: *665 Amsterdam Av.*
Telephone: *212-665-5348*
Website: *gennaronyc.com*
Subway: *1/2/3 to 96th Street*

This cash-only Italian restaurant is more walk than talk. The ambience is relaxed and the menu is straightforward. However, what it lacks in complexity and innovation it makes up for in flavor.

The cuisine is classic Italian, using high-end ingredients, and relying on flavor more than creativity.

Prices range from a basic pasta with tomato sauce ($12) to the homemade veal ravioli in tomato cream sauce ($19.50). The rest of entrées are largely meat based ($18 to $37) with a few seafood options too.

Stay

Jazz on the Park
Address: 36 West 106 Street
Telephone: 212-932-600
Website: jazzhostels.com
Subway: B/C to 103rd Street or 110th Street

A solid budget option can be found at Jazz on the Park. This hostel has private and shared rooms from $70 to $200.

A coffee shop is onsite, and outdoor terraces and a basement with regular events makes this a good place to meet others, if travelling alone.

Free lockers, storage, maps, towels, and house keeping are included, and coin-operated washing machines

Toms Restaurant
Open: *Sun to Wed 6:00am to 1:30am; Thurs to Sat: 24/7*
Address: *2880 Broadway*
Telephone: *212-864-6137*
Website: *tomsrestaurant.net*
Subway: *1 to 116th Street*

If you recognize the awning of Tom's Restaurant, don't doubt yourself. This family owned restaurant from the 1940s is famed for its appearance as Monk's Diner, the regular meeting spot for the characters on the show Seinfeld.

are on site as well.

NYLO
Address: 2178 Broadway
Telephone: 212-362-1100
Website: nylohotels.com/nyc
Subway: 1 to 79th Street

This 4-star hotel dubs itself as embodying "signature urban, industrial design with the energy, color and fashions of New York's Jazz Era." NYLO prides itself on offering the most comfortable beds on the market, and most rooms have large open windows providing great views of the surrounding area. Rooms range from $350 to $700 per night.

While the food here is nothing to write home about, the experience is worthwhile. It's a classic old-style diner with various omelets breakfast options and sandwiches ($8 to $12).

Many people, including the local college students come here for high calorie snacks like French Fries, and their true specialties, the giant malted milk shakes ($6).

With reasonable prices, it's a good place to go for to a relaxed atmosphere.

Hotel Beacon
Address: 2130 Broadway
Telephone: 212-787-1100
Website: beaconhotel.com
Subway: 1/2/3 to 72nd Street

While this is the official hotel of the Beacon Theatre and geared towards audience members, there is no reason to dismiss the option to stay here even if you don't plan on seeing any performances at the Beacon.

Rooms and suites are available with ample size, and kitchenettes, some of which over look Central Park. Standard rooms begin at around $300 and suites climb up to about $450 per night.

Upper East Side

The residents of the Upper East Side work primarily downtown in the commercial and financial industries. It is one of the most affluent neighborhoods in NYC, with well-kept streets to wander around.

Unlike most neighborhoods in the city, the Upper East Side has always been inhabited by the people in the upper echelons of society.

As the area turned from farmland to mansions beside Central Park, people like Andrew Carnegie, Henry Clay Frick, and the Rockefellers were some of the first inhabitants. The only remaining mansion is Gracie Mansion, which has been the home of most NYC mayors since 1942.

The population now is mostly white, with more Jews and Republicans than most of the rest of the areas in NYC. A number of cultural institutions and museums are based in the Upper East Side and all offer something new and interesting.

See and Do

Solomon R. Guggenheim Museum

4/5/6 to 86th Street

guggenheim.org/new-york

Sun to Wed & Fri 10:00am to 5:45pm; Sat 10:00am to 7:45pm. Closed Thurs.

1071 5th Avenue

Ad: $25, Stu & sen: $18, Under 12s: Free

In operation since 1939, the Guggenheim Museum is known for housing some of the most respected and prized contemporary art in the world.

The building itself is a magnificent piece of artwork. Designed by Frank Lloyd Wright, it is cylindrical, and wider at the top than it is the bottom. There is a ramp, which wraps around creating a walking coil.

The structure of the museum lends to displaying artwork in a particular, and often chronological, way.

There are permanent collections, but it's best known for the larger exhibitions that take up the majority of the space.

On Saturdays from 5:45pm to 7:45pm, the museum is pay-as-you-wish

Neighborhood Guide: Upper East Side

Metropolitan Museum of Art

 1 to 66th Street

 metmuseum.org

 Sun to Thur 10:00am to 5:30pm; Fri & Sat 10:00am to 9:00pm.

 1000 Fifth Avenue

 Ad: $25, Sen: $17, Stu: $12, Child (under 12): Free

Known locally as The Met, this museum is the largest art museum in the United States and has been in operation since 1872.

There are 17 curatorial departments and the permanent collection has over two million works from all over the world.

The Met is situated along Central Park, and the inside boasts massive glass walls into which natural light floods.

Additionally, there is a Roof Garden which exhibits art, has a café and bar, and some of the best views of Central Park and the skyline in Manhattan.

The temporary exhibitions at The Met are usually very well-done and should be looked into before going. As the place is enormous, it's best to enter with a plan as to not get lost.

Frick Collection

 6 to 68th Street

 Tues to Sat 10:00am to 6:00pm; Sun 11:00am to 5:00pm

 1 E 70th Street

 Ad: $20, Sen: $15, Stu: $10, Under 10s: No entry, Sun 11:00am to 1:00pm: pay-as-you-wish

 frick.org

Henry Frick was a famous art collector who moved to New York in 1905 and leased the Vanderbilt house at 640 Fifth Avenue. When he did so, a lot of his artwork came with him.

The museum today is in Frick's former residence and many of the pieces of artwork are supposedly arranged in their original formation.

92nd Street Y

 6 to 96th Street

 212-415-5500

 1395 Lexington Avenue

 92y.org

Having begun in 1874 as the Young Men's Hebrew Association, the 92nd Street Y has morphed into a cultural institution that serves various races, faiths, and ethnic groups. The venue hosts a wide range of programs – lectures, concerts, discussions, dances, readings, screenings, and others. Well-known people such as Rachel Maddow and Ira Glass have been guests in events in the past. Check the schedule for events.

Eat

Serendipity 3
Open: *Sun to Thurs 11:30am to midnight; Fri & Sat 11:30am to 1:00am*
Address: *225 E 60th Street*
Telephone: *212-838-3531*
Website: *serendipity3.com*
Subway: *N/Q/R to 59th Street Lexington Ave*

New York's first coffee house boutique, Serendipity 3 opened its doors in 1954. Since then, it's drawn celebrities, neighborhood residents, and visitors alike for its rich delicacies.

While many go for the decadent entrées such as the Bi-Sensual Burger ($23), others enjoy the unique coffee-inspired drinks. They're particularly famous for the Serendipitous Hot Chocolate ($8).

Serependity 3 also serves the world's most expensive sundae, the Golden Opulence Sundae for $1,000; the restaurant claims to sell one per month.

Pastrami Queen
Open: *Daily 10:00am to 10:00pm*
Address: *1125 Lexington Avenue*
Telephone: *212-734-1500*
Website: *pastramiqueen.com*
Subway: *4/6 to 77th Street*

Usually when people think of Zagat-rated eateries they think of upscale dining. However, Pastrami Queen has dedicated its service to preparing the traditional Jewish delights that have made them a renowned restaurant. With meat sandwiches the size of small children, buying the $18 sandwiches can be justified and they can certainly be shared.

Stay

Carlyle Hotel
Address: *35 E 76th Street*
Telephone: *212-744-1600*
Website: *rosewoodhotels.com/en/the-carlyle-new-york*
Subway: *6 to 77th Street*

This landmark hotel epitomizes luxury. Named after a Scotsman, Thomas Carlyle, the Art Deco styles provide an up-class environment for its guests. It has 193 rooms and suites, many of which have beautiful views of Central Park. Rooms are some of the most expensive in the city, starting above $550. The even pricier options go for upwards of $15,000.

The Franklin
Address: *164 East 87th St*
Telephone: *800-607-4009*
Website: *franklinhotel.com*
Subway: *4/5/6 to 86th Street*

A reasonably priced mid-range option is The Franklin. Rooms are priced from $200. The rooms are not particularly spacious, but they are indeed comfortable. It's often considered a romantic option, making it more suitable for couples.

Services include: a European buffet breakfast, wine and artisanal cheese reception, and 24-hour coffees.

Neighborhood Guide: Midtown

Midtown

Midtown is the idyllic place that most people visualize when they hear the words "New York City." Between Times Square, the Empire State Building, Rockefeller Center, and Broadway, this area is a tourist's mecca.

During the day, the streets and sidewalks are overtaken by bodies in every direction. From people in the business, commercial, and financial sectors going between meetings, to tourists treading back and forth between museums, stores, and other sightseeing attractions.

In the evening, the neighborhood epitomizes one of NYC's main slogans, "The City That Never Sleeps." The nightlife comes out in full swing and the buildings light up in all their pride and glory. While many New Yorkers, due to their desensitization, will tell you that Midtown is over-rated and there is more of NYC to see, it's still an essential part of the NYC experience, and not to be over-looked.

See and Do

The Empire State Building

If one skyscraper were to embody NYC, most people would agree it is the Empire State Building.

Since 1931, this 102-story building has enamored most of the world. For 40 years it stood as the world's tallest building but has since fallen in rank and is no longer even in the top 30.

The architectural design is representative of the Art Deco style and it has been designated a National Historic Landmark and one of the Seven Wonders of the Modern World.

Due to the building opening during the unfortunate time of the Great Depression, it took 20 years until it became profitable and inhabited.

Now, the Empire State Building houses 1,000 businesses and even has its own zip code.

The building can be visited, and the 86th floor observation deck is one of the most popular observatories in the world. For an additional fee, it is also possible to get to the 102nd floor (though we wouldn't recommend this as the view is the same and there is glass in the way). The lines tend to be long, and visitors can pay a fee to move to the front of the line.

 N/Q/R/D/F to 34th Street – Herald Square

 Daily 8:00am to 2:00am

 350 Fifth Avenue

 Main Deck, Ad: $37, Sen: $35, Child (6 to 12): $31, No wait: $65; Both Decks, Ad: $57, Sen: $55, Child (6 to 12): $51, No wait: $85

 esbnyc.com

MoMA

 E/M to 53rd Street; B/D/F/M to Rockefeller Center    moma.org

 Saturdays to Thursdays from 10:30am to 5:00pm; Fridays from 10:30am to 8:00pm   11 W 53rd St

 Adults: $25, Seniors (Over 65): $18, Students: $14, Children (Under 16): Free

The Museum of Modern Art (MoMA) is renowned for housing some of the most important modern art in the world.

Though it's been in operation since the early 1900s, renovations in 1983 and 2002 have doubled its original gallery size and created an open and modern structure.

The permanent collections are considered some of the best in world with famous artists such as Paul Cezanne, Marc Chagall, Salvador Dali, Frida Kahlo, Claude Monet, Henri Matisse, Andy Warhol, Pablo Picasso, Jackson Pollock, Vincent Van Gogh, and countless others.

Temporary collections are usually regarded highly and appropriately timed.

Additionally, there are numerous film exhibitions and events held throughout the year.

For those interested in contemporary art, the MoMA is an excellent place to spend half of a day.

Times Square

Times Square is a tourist's mecca; it is a commercial intersection that goes from West 42nd to West 47th Street and convenes at Broadway.

It is Times Square that has given NYC its reputation as the 'City of Light' and it is certainly a sight to be seen.

At most times of the day, this intersection is flooded with people – many tourists as well as people in the business and entertainment industry.

The area is also known as the Theater District, as the surrounding streets house most of the Broadway musicals and plays.

The TKTS booth at the northern end of Times Square is a good place to go for discounted theater tickets: sometimes they can be up to 50% off.

Times Square is home to Planet Hollywood, M&M's World, the Disney Store, and The Hard Rock Café.

We recommend experiencing Times Square during the nighttime to get the full effect of the lights and atmosphere.

Bryant Park

Bryant Park is a small park in the center of Manhattan. It's a serene place in the midst of skyscrapers.

During the 1970s, the area was dangerous – a meeting place for gangs and drug dealers. However, in 1980, the Bryant Park Restoration Corporation sought to make the area safer and has since done a good job.

During warmer months, it is as a common lunch spot for midtown workers. Kiosks serve sandwiches and salads.

Free Ping-Pong is available and there are a number of events held here, such as

 D/F/7 to Bryant Park

 Opens at 7:00am daily. Closing times: Jan to Mid-Mar 10:00pm; Mar 8:00pm; Apr 10:00pm; May 11:00pm; June to Sep, Mon to Fri 12:00am, Weekends 11:00pm; Oct to Dec 10:00pm.

Fifth Avenue and W. 42nd Street

bryantpark.org

film screenings and free yoga classes in the summer. In the winter, an ice skating rink opens in the space.

St. Patrick's Cathedral

 E/M to 53rd Street

 Tours begin at 10:00am

 5th Avenue and 50th Street

 Free

 saintpatricks cathedral.org

This neo-gothic cathedral church stands out in NYC among the skyscrapers and modern buildings.

The land under the cathedral was purchased in 1810 by a Jesuit community who then built a school. The cathedral was designed in 1858 but was not completed until 1878 due to the Civil War.

The cathedral is the seat of the archbishop of the Roman Catholic Archdiocese of New York and it can accommodate up to 3,000 people. There are stained glass windows, Roman sculptures, and various other pieces of artwork along the interior.

Take a peek inside, or enjoy a free tour.

Neighborhood Guide: Midtown

Grand Central Terminal

 4/5/6/S/7 to Grand Central 42nd Street

 Daily 5:30am to 2:00am

 89 E 42nd Street

 Audio tours - Ad: $9, Stu, sen, mil and child: $7; Guided tours - Ad: $30, Stu, sen, mil and child: $20

 grandcentral terminal.com

Although this is a regular commuter stop for many coming from Westchester and Connecticut, it's also an architectural and historical landmark. With over 44 platforms today, it has more platforms than any railroad station in the world.

In 1871, the Grand Central Depot was opened to service the smaller railroads of the time. The original facilities were demolished at the turn of the century and two architectural firms teamed up to design the Beaux-Arts facility.

Various institutions and businesses have cycled through Grand Central, including art galleries, stores, and restaurants.

The Main Concourse tends to draw the most tourists. In the center is a famous golden brass clock atop an information booth which serves as the most popular meeting place for people. The ceiling is a teal sky scape with constellations; it is entirely inaccurate, yet artistic nonetheless.

There are two ways to tour Grand Central. You can take an excellent audio tour daily from 9:00am to 6:00pm. Alternatively, a guided tour is offered daily at 12:30pm.

Rockefeller Center

 B/D/F/M to 47-50th Streets; E/M to 50th Street

 Daily 7:00am to 12:00am

 45 Rockefeller Plaza

 Tour: $25; Tour + Top of the Rock: $50

 rockefellercenter.com

This 22-acre complex of 19 commercial buildings was declared a National Historic Landmark in 1987. It was the largest private building project ever undertaken at the time.

Used during WWII primarily for British Intelligence, the current center still houses the original Art Deco office buildings, as well as the Time-Life Building, McGraw-Hill, and Fox News headquarters, NBC studios, and various other renowned facilities.

Radio City Music Hall, famous for the presentation of the "Radio Christmas Music Spectacular," is an emblem of tradition here.

Other prominent features include the ice-skating rink plaza, open during winter months, and Lee Lawrie's sculpture "Atlas" can also be visited on the premises.

Tours are held every half hour beginning at 10:00am and go until midnight (except 6:00pm to 7:00pm) and are priced at $20 per person.

It's also home to Top of the Rock (see the next page).

New York Public Library

D/F/7 to Bryant Park

Daily 8:00am to 2:00am

Fifth Avenue and W. 42nd Street

Free

nypl.org

The NYPL has several locations throughout the city; however, the main building is located at Bryant Park. It is the largest public library system in the United States with 88 neighborhood branches and over 51 million items.

The combined public and private funding that the NYPL receives gives it innovative freedom and resources for its visitors.

Neighborhood Guide: Midtown

Top of The Rock

 B/D/F/M to 47-50th Streets; E/M to 50th Street

 Daily 8:00am to 12:00am

 30 Rockefeller Plaza

 Ad: $36, Child: $30, Sen: $34; Twice in one day Ad: $54 and Child: $43

 topoftherock nyc.com

Although the Empire State Building has views of the city, the experience of going to the Top of Rockefeller Plaza offers, in our opinion, the best views of anywhere in the NYC area.

Upon entering, you'll go through a mezzanine exhibit detailing the story of Rockefeller Center and the Top of the Rock. Interactive components such as the beam walk put you in the shoes of the people who constructed the building.

After a short video, you'll enter the sky shuttle that will take you to the top.

At the top is an indoor space with comfortable seating and floor-to-ceiling windows where you can enjoy remarkable views.

An outdoor section, complete with binoculars, adds to the experience.

Finally, a photographer is always on site to take photographs.

Eat

Ess-A-Bagel
Open: *Mon to Fri 6:00am to 9:00pm; Weekends 6:00am to 5:00pm*
Address: *831 3rd Avenue*
Telephone: *212-980-1010*
Website: *ess-a-bagel.com*
Subway: *E to Lexington Avenue 53rd Street*

Many would contend that Ess-a-Bagel has the best bagels in the entire city. The original location was established in 1976 on 21st Street, but the Midtown option provides the same selection and quality. The owners came from Austrian families, where baking was a highly respected tradition.

The bagels are boiled to perfection, and there is a wide range of spreads to top them. Additionally, their pastries, muffins, cookies, and other treats will please a sweet tooth.

Sushi Yasuda
Open: *Mon to Fri noon to 2:00pm, 6:00pm to 10:00pm, Sat 6:00pm to 10:00pm*
Address: *204 E 43rd Street*
Telephone: *212-972-1001*
Website: *sushiyasuda.com*
Subway: *4/5/6/S/7 to Grand Central 42nd Street*

Open since 1999, three founders – Naomichi Yasuda, Shige Akimoto, and Scott Rosenberg – have been successfully satisfying the sushi cravings of New Yorkers and visitors alike. The ingredients are local and the menu changes regularly. It is likely that you'll spend over $100 per person, but many say this is the best sushi they have ever eaten.

The Halal Guys
Open: *Daily 10:00am to 4:00pm* Address: *53rd Street & 6th Av*
Website: *53rdand6th.com*
Subway: *B/D/E to 7th Avenue; E/M to 53rd Street*

Halal food carts are a common fixture in NYC, but

Neighborhood Guide: Midtown

The Halal Guys have created a name for themselves that supersedes the rest. They are open notoriously late and have served many drunken New Yorkers.

Totto Ramen
Open: *Mon to Wed 11:45am to 3:00pm and 5:30pm to midnight, Thurs and Fri 11:45 am to 3:00pm and 6:00pm to midnight, Sat 12:30pm to midnight, Sun 4:30pm to 10:30pm*
Address: *248 E 52nd Street*
Telephone: *212-582-0052*
Website: *tottoramen.com*
Subway: *A/C/E to 50th Street*

Although Ramen is traditionally a Japanese noodle soup dish, New Yorkers have fallen in love, giving it a separate cuisine category in their city.

Totto Ramen is a popular spot for a reliable bowl. There is a wide variety and customizable options are

available as well.

Bar Americain
Open: *Sun to Thurs 5:00pm to 10:00pm, Fri 5:00pm to 11:00pm and Sat 4:30pm to 11:00pm*
Address: *152 W 52nd Street*
Telephone: *212-265-9700*
Website: *baramericain.com/nyc/*
Subway: *B/D/E to 7th Avenue; 1 to 50th Street*

Celebrity chef Bobby Flay is the renowned chef behind Bar Americain – an American brasserie with bold flavors. Large appetizers like Spicy Tuna Tartare ($17) are great for sharing. Decadent entrées like Duck Confit with sweet and Sour Apricots ($35) and Gulf Shrimp & Grits with ham, green onions and garlic ($13) can be had, along with steaks and dishes of the day.

Stay

Pod 39
Address: *145 E 39th Street*
Telephone: *212-865-5700*
Website: *thepodhotel.com*
Subway: *4/5/6 to 42nd Street*

An option on the cheaper side suitable to some younger travelers is Pod 39. A modern lodging option with a café, bar, and playroom on-site, it provides small but comfortable rooms. Rooms vary in size and amenities but most include Wi-Fi and personal climate control. Rooms start at $150 to $200 per night.

The St. Regis
Address: *2 East 55th Street*
Telephone: *212-753-4500*
Website: *stregisnewyork.com*
Subway: *E/M to 5th Avenue 53rd Street*

One of the most expensive and luxurious hotels in NYC is the St. Regis. The hotel originally opened in 1904 by John Jacob Astor IV on 55th Street and 5th Avenue.

In 1960 it was bought by ITT Sheraton and was extensively remodeled and renovated in 1991. While it is true to its origins of beaux-arts style, the renovations make it a place to feel like royalty.

With butler service top-level hospitality, you can rent rooms beginning at $600. They climb up to $1,000 or more depending on the style.

Neighborhood Guide: Chelsea

Chelsea

Chelsea is located in the West Side of Manhattan, bordering the Hudson River. This is one of the city's premier art locations.

The name Chelsea was derived from the manor of Chelsea in London, home to English lawyer and philosopher, Thomas More.

Chelsea began to be developed in 1827. While Benjamin Moore sought to build well-designed residential buildings, industrial facilities began opening along the Hudson River.

Increased industrialization led to immigrants coming to Chelsea to work at the factories. Thus, tenements crammed with dwellers sparked riots and violence.

Theater, as a means of frustrated expression, came to the area and West 23rd Street was originally the center of theater in the US.

During World War II, a large amount of uranium for the Manhattan Project (atomic bomb) was stored in factories on 20th Street. The decontamination of the facilities did not take place until the 1990s.

Currently Chelsea is known for its artistic crowd as it is the epicenter of NYC galleries. It is also known to have a large LGBT population and prides itself of upscale diversity.

Many of the old industrial factories have been converted into places to shop and entertain, adding to the gentrification of the area.

See and Do

Rubin Museum of Art

The Rubin Museum of Art houses a collection of Himalayan and Tibetan art.

Opened in 2004, this relatively new museum has gained critical acclaim for advancing the study and interest in Himalayan arts.

On and off-site educational activities have made this institution be respected for its commitment to cultural education

 F/M/A/C/E/L/1/2/3 to 14th Street

 Opens at 11:00am. Closes: Mon & Thur 5:00pm; Wed 9:00pm; Fri 10:00pm; Sat & Sun 6:00pm. Closed on Tues.

 150 W 17th Street

 Ad: $15 / Stu & Sen: $10 / Child (Under 12): Free

🌐 rubinmuseum.org

Chelsea Market

 A/C/E/L to 14th Street

 Mon to Sat 7:00am to 2:00am; Sun 8:00am to 10:00pm (some shops close early)

 75 9th Avenue

 chelseamarket.com

In the former Nabisco factory complex lies Chelsea Market – a square block sized complex that has restaurants and shops that could occupy you for an entire day.

Events, such as pop-up shops, art shows, and concerts, occur throughout the year.

Food tours are also available, which must be organized in advance, but this is a great way to not miss the many tastes and the history behind the market.

We think this is a must-do on any NYC itinerary. There is no charge to enter the market.

The High Line

 L at 14th Street; A/C/E at 14th or 34th; 1/2/3 at 14th or 34th Street

 Dec to Mar 7:00am to 7:00pm; Apr to May & Oct to Nov 7:00am to 10:00pm; Jun to Sep 7:00am to 11:00pm

 thehighline.org

The High Line is a new addition to NYC, opening in 2009, and has been immensely popular ever since.

This linear park was built on an elevated section of railroad called the West Side Line. It extends from Gansevoort Street to 34th Street and is best experienced from walking one end to the other.

It passes under Chelsea Market – a sizable food hall on 15th Street – where many visitors break for a meal, and over the various art galleries that Chelsea is famed for.

Unique to the High Line are the interesting plants and landscaping that grow over the old train tracks.

Additionally, temporary art installations change throughout the year.

Neighborhood Guide: Chelsea

Chelsea Piers

 A/C/E to 23rd Street   62 Chelsea Piers   chelseapiers.com

Historically Chelsea Piers was where major ships such as the RMS Lusitania and the RMS Titanic landed. Today, its current use is for sport and recreation.

The complex has a health club, day spa, and facilities for nearly every sport imaginable.

It also houses Chelsea Brewing Company, the only micro-brewery in Manhattan. Hours and Prices vary depending on activity.

Galleries

 A/C/E to 23rd Street   Free   chelseagallerymap.com

In recent years, Chelsea has become a mecca for contemporary art galleries. They fill the streets between 18th and 28th and between the avenues of 10th and 11th.

Some of the most notable and prominent galleries in the world have outposts here, such as Agora Gallery, ACA Galleries, David Swirner, Gagosian Gallery and others.

All of them are free to enter and browse, and most are open between 10:00am and 6:00pm, however you should check the hours before going.

Eat

Billy's Bakery
Open: *Mon to Thurs 8:30am to 11.00pm; Fri 8:30am to midnight; Sat 9:00am to midnight; Sun 9:00am to 9:00pm*
Address: *184 9th Avenue*
Telephone: *212-647-9956*
Website: *billysbakerynyc.com*
Subway: *A/C/E to 23rd Street; 1 to 23rd Street*

This 1940s-style bakery began with two guys who met in business school and wanted to share their love of sweets with NYC.

They make a wide range of cakes, pies, cupcakes, and cookies but are particularly known for their incredibly decadent red velvet cake.

However, they don't shy away from more innovative options like the Banana Nutella Cupcake or the chocolate covered pretzel cheesecake.

Murray's Bagels
Open: *Mon to Fri 6:30am to 7:00pm, Sat & Sun 6:30am to 6:30pm*
Address: *242 8th Avenue*
Telephone: *646-638-1335*
Website: *murraysbagelschelsea.com*
Subway: *A/C/E to 23rd Street; 1/2 to 23rd Street*

This famous NYC bagel shop is notorious for not toasting their bagels. Their "no toast rule" derives from their belief that a perfectly fresh and delectable bagel doesn't need toasting.

A simple bagel with cream cheese will run you $3.25, while opting for their classic sandwich, The Traditional – a bagel with nova scotia salmon, cream cheese, beefsteak tomatoes, red onions and capers – will run you up to $11.50.

They also have signature sandwiches like The Rueben – hot corned beef, Swiss cheese, Russian dressing and sauerkraut ($11.95), as well as other classic NYC combinations.

Blossom Restaurant
Open: *Sun 12:00pm to 2:45pm, 5:00pm to 9:00pm, Mon to Thurs midday to 2:45pm, 5:00pm to 9:30pm, Fri & Sat 12:00pm to 2:45pm, 5:00pm to 10:00pm*
Address: *187 9th Avenue*
Telephone: *212-627-1144*
Website: *blossomnyc.com*
Subway: *A/C/E to 23rd Street*

This restaurant began in 2005 in Chelsea with a

mission to bring high-end vegan food to everyone willing to try. While this is geared towards vegans, it has delicious food suitable for all.

Starters include things like Gnocchi (sun-dried tomato, spinach, snow peas, fried leeks, lemon-truffle-cashew sauce) at $16 and Bourekas at $13 - cashew cheese, spinach, hummus, za'atar, olives.

The entrées often are a twist on more traditional meat dishes like the Lasagna (tapioca cheese, ground seitan & tofu, marinara, roasted eggplant, sautéed escarole) at $22.

The Meatball Shop
Open: *Sun to Thur 11:30am to 12:00am; Fri & Sat 11:30am to 1:00am*
Address: *200 9th Avenue*
Telephone: *212-257-4363*
Website: *themeatballshop.com*
Subway: *1/2 to 23rd Street*

The Meatball Shop is a trendy option for high quality food at a reasonable price.

While you can get a traditional Meatball Hero, the place prides itself on the balls themselves, and sells them "naked."

With a choice of beef, pork, chicken, or veggie, and a choice of sauce, you will get 4 meatballs, cheese, and focaccia bread for $8. A range of sides is available to have with the balls or on their own, and sliders can also be made with the locally sourced ingredients.

Stay

Highline Hotel
Address: *180 10th Avenue*
Telephone: *212-929-3888*
Website: *thehighlinehotel.com*
Subway: *A/C/E to 23rd Street*

The Highline Hotel has 60 rooms, but each feels handcrafted. With locally sourced furniture, complimentary lush robes, and complimentary Intelligentsia coffee, the hotel oozes comfort and calm.

Rooms range from 200 to 500 square feet, with views of the Highline, the back garden, or Chelsea's streets. Free Wi-Fi, as well as calls to anywhere in the world are included with the stay. Rooms range from $250 to $650 per night depending on dates and specs.

Chelsea International Hostel
Address: *251 W 20th Street*
Telephone: *212-647-0010*
Website: *chelseahostel.com*
Subway: *A/C/E to 23rd Street*

The premier budget option in NYC is Chelsea Hostel.

This place has no frills. It's your bare bones hostel, good for young people who don't anticipate spending much time in the room. They also offer basic private rooms which are good value.

Rates are fixed and vary on size and time of year, but can be as low as $54 per night for a shared room and private rooms can be found from $75 per night (or from $110 with an en-suite), a deal difficult to beat in Manhattan. They also offer kitchen facilities, lobby internet access, and a free breakfast.

Flatiron

The Flatiron District is named after the iconic Flatiron Building. Before the 1980s, the area was known as the Toy District due to the Toy Center buildings in its location. Since then, it has become much more residential and houses photography offices and publishing companies.

Aside from the Flatiron Building itself, there is the Met Life Tower, which was the tallest building until 1913 when the Woolworth Building downtown was completed.

The neighborhood boundaries are small but there is still a fair amount of exploring that can be done.

See and Do

Flatiron Building

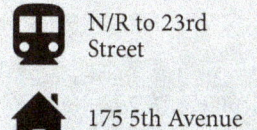

N/R to 23rd Street

175 5th Avenue

This architectural marvel is one of the most photographed buildings in the city. It is currently the headquarters of numerous established publishing companies.

It was designed by Daniel Burnham in a Beaux-Arts style. Since its inception, visitors have come to stare at it in amazement.

Madison Square Park

N/R to 23rd Street

Daily 6:00am to 12:00am

11 Madison Avenue

Free

madisonsquarepark.org

Just across the street from the Flatiron Building is Madison Square Park.

What was once a swampy hunting ground in the 1700s, an army arsenal in the early 1800s, and a farmhouse turned vacant lot until 1847, is now a gorgeous public park.

Various events and festivals are held here throughout the year, and it is also simply a place to enjoy a nice day.

It's also the birthplace of Shake Shack, a popular New York burger stop.

Neighborhood Guide: Flatiron

Museum of Sex

 N/R to 28th Street

 museumofsex.com

 Sun to Thurs 10:30am to 10:00pm; Fri & Sat 10:30am to 11:00pm

 233 5th Avenue

 Monday to Friday before 1:00pm - $17.50. Any other time: $20.50. $2 discount for students/senior/military with valid ID.

The Museum of Sex presents the history, evolution, and cultural constructions of human sexuality.

Founder Daniel Gluck opened up with an exhibit called *NYC Sex: How New York City Transformed Sex in America* and since 2009 has expanded its scope and coverage at the current location.

Eat

Shake Shack
Open: *Mon to Fri 7:30am to 11:00pm, Say & Sun 8:30am to 11:00pm*
Address: *Madison Ave & E 23rd S*
Website: *shakeshack.com*
Subway: *N/R/6 to 23rd Street*

Shake Shack began as a hot dog cart in Madison Square Park in 2001. The classic Shack Burger is made with 100% all-natural Angus beef ($5.29 for a single, $8.09 for a double). They also have a veggie option, the Shroom Burger ($6.99). Fries and dogs are also available but they're known particularly for their Shakes, floats, and custards ($5-$7).

11 Madison Park
Open: *Lunch - Fri to Sun 12:00pm to 1:00pm, Dinner - Mon to Wed 5:30pm to 10:00pm and Thur to Sun 5:30pm to 10:30pm*
Address: *11 Madison Av.*
Telephone: *212-889-0905*
Website: *elevenmadisonpark.com*
Subway: *N/R/6 to 23rd St*

This restaurant is one of the best and most highly regarded in NYC. Rated three stars by the Michelin Guide, the 8 to 10-course tasting menu highlights the natural agricultural advantages and culinary traditions of New York. For $315 per person (tip included), many say this is the best meal of their lives.

Eisenberg's Sandwich Shop
Open: *Weekdays 6:30am to 8:00pm; Sat 9:00am to 6:00pm; Sun 9:00am to 5:00pm*
Address: *174 5th Avenue*
Telephone: *212-675-5096*
Website: *eisenbergsnyc.com*
Subway: *N/R/6 to 23rd St*

This old-style New York Deli features classic red bar stools to eat at the counter. Small two-person tables and chairs line the wall just a few feet behind the counter stools.

For a grab and go breakfast option they have classic Egg Sandwiches ($4 to $5). They're known for their classic simple options like Tuna Melts and Hot Corned Beef Sandwiches ($8 and $12). Also, some say this is the best place to get a traditional Egg Cream – a drink of milk, soda water, and chocolate syrup ($2).

Stay

The Flatiron Hotel
Address: *9 W 26th Street*
Telephone: *212 839-8000*
Website: *flatironhotel.com*
Subway: *N/R to 28th Street*

The 65 rooms at the Flatiron Hotel provide oversized windows and various views of the city. The boutique luxury hotel has Jacuzzi bathtubs, Swiss rainfall showers, and oversized beds. On the roof is Toshi's Penthouse – an events terrace and Toshi's Living Room, a music venue.

Rooms start at $250 but can run up to $600.

Gramercy Park

Gramercy Park is often considered one of the most private and secluded neighborhoods in NYC. This is in part thanks to the private, fenced-in park after which it is named, as well as the exorbitant apartment prices.

The current location was in the middle of a swamp, which in 1831 was developed into a residential area.

Due to zoning laws, the buildings in this area are required to be less than 20 stories. Most the buildings are only 3 to 4 stories high, making the residential area all the quieter and private.

Although it's hardly a haven for tourist attractions, it does provide pleasant strolls and offers a different side to the bustling nature of the rest of the city.

See and Do

Gramercy Park

 6 to 23rd Street

 Between 19th and 20th Street; Between Park Avenue and 3rd Avenue

Gramercy Park is a fenced-in park, which only the residents of the original lots surrounding the park are allowed to enter. In 2012, 383 keys were in circulation.

In the past, the park was opened to the public for one day each year, in the beginning of May. However, due to the influx of visitors, they stopped the event in 2007.

Now, visitors can simply wander the perimeter and imagine an idyllic life inside.

Theodore Roosevelt Birthplace

 6 to 23rd Street

 nps.gov/thrb

 Free

 Wed to Sun 9:00am to 5:00pm

 28 E 20th Street

Theodore Roosevelt was the only United States president to be born in NYC.

The site is visited by guided tours only. Normally there are Park Ranger guided tours on the hour with no tour at noon.

The area is run by the National Park Service, a rarity in NYC.

Neighborhood Guide: Gramercy Park

The Gramercy Theatre

 N/R/6 to 23rd Street   venue.thegramercy theatre.com   127 E 23rd Street

The Gramercy Theatre opened in 1937 as a movie theater and did not start offering different forms of entertainment until 1998. It then began showing off-Broadway theater productions but was shut down in 2004. In 2007, Live Nation purchased the space and it has been turned into a music venue showing a wide range of musical styles.

Vintage Shopping

Gramercy is home to one of the city's highest concentrations of high-end vintage shops. Walking back and forth on some of the streets, you'll come across a lot of used-items stores that have themes and are well curated. While cheaper options like Salvation Army can be found, you'll also come across an array of more expensive vintage clothes.

Eat

Pete's Tavern
Open: *Sun to Wed 11:00am to 2:30am, Thurs 11:00am to 3:00am, Fri and Sat 11:00am to 4:00am*
Address: *129 East 18th Street*
Telephone: *212-473-7676*
Website: *petestavern.com*
Subway: *N/Q/R/4/5/6/L to Union Square*

Having opened in 1869, Pete's Tavern is the oldest continuously operating restaurant in NYC. The menu is Italian-American, with classic seafood, fried, and meat options. One can opt for a simple eggplant parmigiana ($17.75) or have a Veal Scaloppini ($23.75) with a side of French fries or onion rings.

While not all of the combinations prove to be the most sensible, it gives the establishment a unique and distinguished flare.

Irving Farm Coffee Roasters
Open: *Weekdays 7:00am to 8:00pm; Weekends 8:00am to 8:00pm*
Address: *71 Irving Place*
Telephone: *212-995-5252*
Website: *irvingfarm.com*
Subway: *N/Q/R/4/5/6/L to Union Square*

Whether you're just dropping in for a cup of coffee or staying for lunch, this little shop will please anyone's cravings.

From deliciously roasted coffee, to sweet pastries, and fresh salads to sandwiches, Irving Farm Coffee Roasters offers a delicious lunch or beverage option at this original location.

Gramercy Tavern
Open: *Sundays to Thursdays 11:30am to 11:00pm;* *Fridays and Saturdays 11:30am to 12:00am*
Address: *42 E 20th Street*
Telephone: *212-477-0777*
Website: *gramercytavern.com*
Subway: *N/Q/R/4/5/6/L to Union Square*

For a fine dining experience in the neighborhood, it's hard to beat the Gramercy Tavern. The restaurant serves locally-sourced meals throughout the year.

In the tavern, you can order a wide range of dishes a la carte: sea bass, duck leg, lobster broth – you name it, they prepare it to perfection.

The dining room offers both a la carte options and tasting menus, both vegetarian and meat based ($79 to $179). Gratuities are included in meal prices.

Stay

Carlton Arms Hotel
Address: *160 E 25th Street*
Telephone: *212-679-0680*
Website: *carltonarms.com*

Since this building's construction over 100 years ago, it's primarily served as a hotel.

The name of this 54-room establishment plays off the history of the Irish presence in the area during the prohibition era.

A number of artists passed through the hotel in the 1970s and 1980s and the walls still hold some of their murals and fingerprints.

This budget option starts at $130 for one person and a shared bathroom, and goes up to $250 for four people with a private bath.

Gramercy Park Hotel
Address: *2 Lexington Avenue*
Telephone: *212-920-3300*
Website: *gramercyparkhotel.com*
Subway: *6 to 23rd Street*

All the furnishings, both large and small, have been hand-chosen and are highly valued at the 5-Star Gramercy Park Hotel. Many of them come from famous artists, such as Julian Schnabel.

The rooms are composed of vibrant colors reflecting the renaissance revival style of the institution.

The hotel's walls are like a museum; works of Andy Warhol, Jean-Michel Basquiat, Keith Haring, and others are on display in the hallways. Even the on-site dining is some of the best in the city, coming from Danny Meyer's renowned hospitality group. Rooms begin at just less than $500/night and climb to over $1,000.

Guests of this hotel can sign out one of six keys to enter the exclusive gated Gramercy Park.

The Marcel at Gramercy
Address: *201 E 24th Street*
Telephone: *212-696-3800*
Website: *themarcelatgramercy.com*
Subway: *6 to 23rd Street*

The Marcel offers 136 guestrooms, a 10th floor business lounge, and a rooftop terrace with complimentary wine tasting. Rooms are spacious, comfortable and usually fall within the $300 to $400 per night range, though in low season you may find these as low as $150 per night.

Neighborhood Guide: Union Square

Union Square

Although Union Square Park is relatively small in size, it is rich in action, history, and significance. Noted for an equestrian statue of George Washington and other statues, Union Square is known as an epicenter of social and political activism.

Since 1861, Union Square became the site of rallies when it is said a quarter of a million people gathered to rally. In the more recent years, the square has served similar purposes. After the 9/11 attacks, numerous people gathered to mourn in the city park.

It was also a central meeting point for the Occupy Wall Street movement. On any given day protesters and activists can be found on the stairs urging you to hear their cause.

See and Do

Union Square Greenmarket

4/5/6/L to Union Square

Mon, Wed, Fri & Sat 8:00am to 6:00pm

Union Square Park

Free

grownyc.org/greenmarket

In 1976, the greenmarket began with just a few farmers in Union Square. They would sell products to a small number of followers.

The market has since grown into one of the most popular urban markets in the area.

People of all ages come to sample and purchase high-quality farmed goods in the middle of an urban metropolis.

Irving Plaza

 4/5/6/L to Union Square   irvingplaza.com   Varies

 Varies according to shows.   17 Irving Place

This ballroom-style music venue can house over 1,000 patrons. From 1948 to 1976, the space was a Polish-American community center, but in 1978 it was converted into a rock music venue.

Run by Live Nation, the venue showcases a wide range of contemporary musical artists.

Neighborhood Guide: Union Square

Eat

Grey Dog
Open: *Mon to Fri 7:30am to 10:00pm, Sat & Sun 8:15am to 10:00pm*
Address: *90 University Place*
Telephone: *212-414-4739*
Website: *thegreydog.com*
Subway: *N/Q/R/4/5/6/L to Union Square*

The Grey Dog is a reliable place to go with options for everyone. They don't serve up anything super fancy, but what they do make is just what you need. The challah French toast ($10.95) is a favorite, along with the Breakfast Quesadilla ($13.50). The rest of the day, they serve sandwiches, salads, and more. Or, simply get a coffee, tea, or beer.

Nanoosh
Open: *Weekdays 11:00am to 10:00pm; Weekends 12:00pm to 10:00pm*
Address: *111 University Pl.*
Telephone: *212-397-0744*
Website: *nanoosh.com*
Subway: *N/Q/R/4/5/6/L to Union Square*

This small NYC chain delivers Mediterranean food with fresh ingredients at reasonable prices. Soups, salads, wraps, and power food plates give vegetarians and vegans plenty to choose from, while also providing meat lovers with some solid options ($9 to $13). Almost everything is served with warm fresh-baked pita.

5 Napkin Burger
Open: *Weekdays 11:30am to 12:00am; Weekends 10:00am to 12:00am*
Address: *150 E 14th Street*
Telephone: *212-228-5500*
Website: *www.5napkinburger.com*
Subway: *N/Q/R/4/5/6/L to Union Square*

This burger joint offers a range of burgers including the '5 Napkin burger' which is 10 ounces of fresh ground beef, gruyere cheese, and caramelized onions atop a roll ($16). Other options are the Bacon cheddar, the Ahi Tuna, and the Veggie ($14 to $17).

Max Brenner
Open: *Mon to Thur 9:00am to 1:00am, Fri & Sat 9:00am to 2:00am, Sun 9:00am to midnight*
Address: *841 Broadway*
Telephone: *646-467-8803*
Address: *maxbrenner.com*
Subway: *N/Q/R/4/5/6/L to Union Square*

Max Brenner is a place to indulge. The restaurant is all about serving up chocolate in new and different ways. Beverages include the Chocolate Martini – with chocolate, vodka, crème de cacao, and a strawberry ($13.25).

While they have sandwiches, salads, and more, the dessert menu is where imaginations really run wild. You can also opt for things like Dark Chocolate Covered Cherry Waffles ($14) or the popular Chocolate Chunks Pizza (half $9.50, whole $18).

Stay

Hyatt Union Square
Address: *134 4th Avenue*
Telephone: *212-253-1234*
Website: *unionsquare.hyatt.com*
Subway: *N/Q/R/4/5/6/L to Union Square*

This luxury option offers 178 rooms designed by established interior designer Paul Vega. His style combines high-technology designs with natural imagery. In a historic building with modern amenities, this is certainly a traditional combination of the old and the new. From studios to deluxe suites, rooms progress from $470 to $2,300.

The Inn at Irving Place
Address: *56 Irving Place*
Telephone: *212-533-4600*
Website: *innatirving.com*
Subway: *N/Q/R/4/5/6/L to Union Square*

This is a private and somewhat elusive place to stay. There are no signs that are indicators of the location; simply the address is displayed.

With 12 guest rooms, suites, and residences, the designers have taken care to furnish each room carefully with hand-selected antiques.

Rooms range from $445 to $645 per night. Situated on the lovely Irving Place this is a quiet, secluded, and quaint option.

Greenwich Village

Greenwich Village has been referred to as the cultural capital of the world by some. Many call it just "The Village," which indicates a location of progressive, and sometimes edgy, perspectives.

"The Village" was the starting place of the Bohemian movement, an epicenter of LGBT acceptance, and the start of the counter culture movement of the 1960s.

While the neighborhood has greatly changed in the past few decades due to gentrification, the remnants of the past movements can still be seen and felt in the general area.

New York University, one of the country's largest private non-profit institutions with over 53,000 students is in the heart of Greenwich Village, as are other smaller universities such as Yeshiva University, The New School, and The Cooper Union.

The presence of all of these universities has contributed to rising rent and living costs, and gentrification.

See and Do

Grey Art Gallery

 N/R to 8th Street; 6 to Astor Place; A/B/C/D/E/F/M to West 4th Street

 nyu.edu/greyart

 Suggested $5

 Tues, Thur & Fri 11:00am to 6:00pm; Wed 11:00am to 8:00pm; Sat 11:00am to 5:00pm

 100 Washington Square East

The Grey Art Gallery, NYU's fine arts museum is right next to Washington Square Park. The idea behind the exhibitions is to preserve, study, document, and display representations of human culture. There are exhibitions of all different mediums of artwork throughout the year.

Comedy Cellar

 A/B/C/D/E/F/M to West 4th Street

 212-254-3480

 comedycellar.com

 117 Macdougal Street

The Comedy Cellar is a high-end comedy club in NYC that was set up in 1982 by Bill Grundfest. Some regular performers include Colin Quinn, Jim Norton, Darrell Hammon, Louis C.K., Dave Chapelle, and countless others. There are numerous comedy shows held nightly and they vary in price based on performance and time.

Neighborhood Guide: Greenwich Village

Washington Square Park

A/B/C/D/E/F/M to West 4th Street

Open 24/7

Washington Square Park

Free

nycgovparks.org/parks/washington-square-park

In addition to Union Square Park, Washington Square Park has served as a meeting place for cultural activity and protest.

While nearly all of the buildings surrounding the park belong to NYU, making it NYU's makeshift campus, it attracts people from all walks of life.

The two main features of the park are the arch and the fountain. The Washington Square Arch was conceived in 1889 to celebrate the 100-year anniversary of George Washington first becoming president.

The result was a wooden arch built north of the park and its popularity led to architect Stanford White designing a permanent marble arch modeled off of Paris's Arc de Triomphe in 1892, which stands prominently in the park today.

The central fountain was renovated in 1934 to serve as a wading pool. As the temperatures become warmer, the fountain fills with water and residents and tourists alike come and play in the water.

When the fountain is empty it serves as a venue for prominent street performers to come and showcase their acts in front of large crowds. Whether it's a man playing a saxophone, a full jazz ensemble, or a circus act, street performers can almost always be found all around the park.

Margo Feiden Galleries

 N/R to 8th Street; 6 to Astor Place   alhirschfeld.com   Free

 Mon to Fri 9:00am to 6:00pm   15 East 9th Street

The Margo Feiden Galleries house a collection of Al Hirschfeld's drawings, paintings, lithographs, and various other artworks. The work is found inside a Stanford White Townhouse in The Village and provides a comprehensive overview of 75 years of work.

Neighborhood Guide: Greenwich Village

Blue Note

A/B/C/D/E/F/M to West 4th Street

212-475-0049

131 W 3rd Street

bluenote.net/newyork

Blue Note is one of the most distinguished jazz clubs in New York City, and arguably the world.

Some of the most famous artists like Chick Corea, Chris Botti, Liza Minelli, Tony Bennett, Stevie Wonder, and various others have performed here over the years.

Expect music every evening at 8:00pm and 10:30pm. Cover charges vary, and food and drinks are served.

Eat

Artichoke Basille's
Open: *Sun to Thur 11:00am to 4:00am, Fri & Sat 11:00am to 5:00am*
Address: *111 Macdougal Street*
Telephone: *646-278-6100*
Website: *artichokepizza.com*
Subway: *A/B/C/D/E/F/M to West 4th Street*

Artichoke Basille's is well-known for their Spinach artichoke slice, which at $4 seems expensive. However, after one of these big slices you'll feel like you don't need another meal in days.

Other options, including the popular Margarita, the anchovy pizza, or crab pizza, all provide a sizable slice that will leave your mouth watering.

Mamoun's
Open: *Daily 11:00am to 5:00am*
Address: *119 Macdougal Street*
Telephone: *212-674-8685*
Website: *mamouns.com*
Subway: *A/B/C/D/E/F/M to West 4th Street*

For a cheap, quick, and grab and go option, it's hard to find one better than Mamoun's.

Years ago they became famous for their cheap falafel sandwiches, which cost $4. Other classic Mediterranean options like tabbouleh, baba ganouj, are all available at reasonable prices. Cash only.

Lupa Osteria Romana
Open: *Sun to Thurs 11:30am to 11:00pm; Fri & Sat 11:30am to midnight*
Address: *170 Thompson Street*
Telephone: *212-982-5089*
Website: *luparestaurant.com*
Subway: *A/B/C/D/E/F/M to West 4th Street*

Mario Batali, Joe Bastianich, Mark Ladner, Jason Denton, all have a share in this establishment. The food is traditionally Roman with some New York influences.

It is by no means cheap, but for the level of prestige these chefs and restaurateurs have, the prices are reasonable.

Prices range from the Lamb Scottadito with Gnocchi Alla Romana ($37) or Octopus with Swiss Chard and Potato ($29) to the Spaghetti Aglio e Olio ($14).

Third Rail Coffee
Open: *Mon to Fri 7:00am to 8:00pm; Sat & Sun 8:00am to 8:00pm*
Address: *240 Sullivan Street*
Telephone: *646-580-1240*
Website: *thirdrailcoffee.com*
Subway: *A/B/C/D/E/F/M to West 4th Street*

Some of the best coffee

Neighborhood Guide: Greenwich Village

can be found at Third Rail Coffee. They brew Counter Culture Coffee and rotate guest coffees regularly. A small, but tasty selection of pastries and snacks are available on site.

Joe's Pizza
Open: *Sun to Thur 10:00am to 4:00am; Fri to Sun 10:00am to 5:00am*
Address: *7 Carmine Street*
Telephone: *212-366-1182*
Website: *joespizzanyc.com*
Subway: *A/B/C/D/E/F/M to West 4th Street*

Owner Joe Pozzouli, after which Joe's is named, was

from Naples, Italy and began serving pizza to New Yorkers in 1975.

This place is often rated as one of the best pizzas in New York. Joe's serves authentic pizza. There are 3 options: plain cheese, fresh mozzarella or Sicilian square. Pies are $20-$24 and slices are $3.

Stay

Washington Square Hotel
Address: *103 Waverly Place*
Telephone: *212-777-9515*
Website: *washingtonsquarehotel.com*
Subway: *A/B/C/D/E/F/M to West 4th Street*

The Washington Square Hotel has historically been a meeting place for writers, artists, and visitors. The 152 rooms have been modernized, but still have remnants of the past. Rooms have terry cloth bathrobes and granite-top vanity tables along with traditional amenities. Rooms typically range from $350 to $550.

The Marlton Hotel
Address: *5 W 8th Street*
Telephone: *212-321-0100*
Website: *marltonhotel.com*
Subway: *A/B/C/D/E/F/M to West 4th Street*

Even though The Marlton Hotel doesn't necessarily have the most spacious rooms, the architecture is certainly something to be admired. The rooms and other facilities have been tastefully designed. Rooms start at $350.

Lafayette House
Address: *38 E 4th Street*
Telephone: *212-505-8100*
Website: *lafayettenyc.com*
Subway: *N/R to 8th Street; 6 to Astor Place*

Situated in a 'brown stone' constructed in 1848, this lodging option offers rooms with antique furnishings and homey features like a fireplace. Staying here will give you the feeling of living in an upscale apartment and give you an idyllic vision of what it means to be a New Yorker. Rooms start at about $400 per night.

Neighborhood Guide: West Village

West Village

Although some do not distinguish between Greenwich Village and the West Village and group them together, in recent years the West Village has created an identity for itself separate from its surroundings.

It earned the informal nickname "Little Bohemia" in 1916 and has been a constant source of housing for artists.

The neighborhood is entirely off of the Manhattan grid, and the streets are narrower and laid out in different formations than the rest of most of the city.

This is an area seldom visited by tourists.

See and Do

Stonewall Inn

 1 to Christopher Street; A/B/C/D/E/F/M to West 4th Street

 Daily 2:00pm to 4:00am

 53 Christopher Street

 thestonewallinnnyc.com

This bar in NYC was the site of the Stonewall riots of 1969 – violent demonstrations by the gay community. Consequently, it is known to be a founding place for the gay liberation movement.

Renovated and reopened in 1999 by the Greenwich Village Society for Historic Preservation, it's been declared a National Historic Landmark and has developed into hosting musical artists, drag shows, cabaret, and more.

Westbeth Artists Community

 1 to Christopher Street

 westbeth.org

 Free

 Wed to Sun midday to 6:00pm

 55 Bethune Street

This non-profit housing complex was designed to offer living and working space for artists in NYC.

It was the site of Bell Laboratories from 1868-1966 and opened in 1970 for artists of various backgrounds.

Galleries and performance spaces are situated throughout the space and many notable and prominent artists have lived and worked there in the past.

Neighborhood Guide: West Village

Eat

McNulty's Tea & Coffee
Open: *Mon to Sat 10:00am to 9:00pm; Sun 1:00pm to 7:00pm*
Address: *109 Christopher St.*
Telephone: *212-242-5351*
Website: *mcnultys.com*
Subway: *1 to Christopher St.*

Many consider McNulty's a New York cultural institution. With over 100 varieties of loose-leaf tea, and old ceilings and walls, the odors that reach the sidewalk beckon visitors to see this establishment that has been around since 1895.

Whether you're planning on buying a or just browsing, this is an interesting and unique place to visit.

The Cornelia Street Café
Open: *Sun to Thur 10:00am to 11:45pm, Fri & Sat 10:00am to 1:00am*
Address: *29 Cornelia Street*
Telephone: *212-989-9319*
Website: *corneliastreetcafe.com*
Subway: *A/B/C/D/E/F/M to West 4th Street*

The Cornelia Street Café doubles as a restaurant and a literary venue. Since 1922, the space has been devoted to presenting a variety of arts. People like Suzanne Vega and Oliver Sacks have performed and presented here, and there is normally more than one performance each night.

The menu is upscale café food. Starters are available like a Eggs Benedict with Smoked Salmon Plate ($14). More decadent options like the Magret of Long Island Duck ($34) or Thai Bouillabaisse ($26) are also on offer.

Magnolia Bakery
Open: *Sun to Thur 10:00am to 10:30pm; Fri & Sat 10:00am to 11:30pm*
Address: *401 Bleecker Street*
Telephone: *212-462-2572*
Website: *magnoliabakery.com*
Subway: *1 to Christopher St.*

This famous bakery opened in 1996 at the Bleecker Street location in the West Village.

While it makes a range of desserts, it has become known for its irresistible rich cupcakes. They have a classic vanilla and chocolate, not to be overlooked, as well as specialty creative cupcakes like the Hummingbird – banana, pineapple, and pecan cake with cream cheese icing ($3.95). Another popular choice is the banana bread pudding.

One If By Land, Two If By Sea
Open: *Sun to Thur 5:30pm to 9:30pm; Fri & Sat 5:15pm to 10:30pm*
Address: *17 Barrow Street*
Telephone: *212-255-8659*
Website: *oneifbyland.com*
Subway: *1 to Christopher St.*

At this fine dining establishment, the 3-course prix fixe menu is $100 or you can do the tasting menu of 7 courses for $150. It is considered one of the most romantic restaurants in all of NYC, serving dishes like spiced beet tartare with ginger, black plum, and bonito aioli and Maine Lobster bakes. The bold red walls and charming ambience make this a popular destination for marriage proposals and anniversaries.

Neighborhood Guide: West Village

Stay

The Jane
Address: *113 Jane Street*
Telephone: *212-924-6700*
Website: *thejanenyc.com*
Subway: *A/C/E/L to 14th Street*

The Jane was built by the same architect that designed Ellis Island's immigration station. It began as the facility for the American Seaman's Friend Society Sailor's Home and Institute in 1908 and housed Titanic survivors in 1912 for a long period of time. During the 1980s and the 1990s the hotel was a meeting place for people involved in the Bohemia movement.

Now, rooms have rainfall showerheads, marble sinks, and river views and terraces, while still keeping stylistic remnants of the past. Rooms are small and compact, starting at $150.

The Standard, High Line
Address: *848 Washington St.*
Telephone: *212-645-4646*
Website: *standardhotels.com/high-line*
Subway: *A/C/E/L to 14th St.*

This modern chain option has 338 rooms with floor-

to-ceiling walls that allow you to marvel at the Hudson River. Comfortable beds are fitted with Italian sheets and the hotel has large bath towels. There is a 24-hour fitness center, a seasonal rooftop bar, complimentary bikes, and an ice skating rink in the winter.

Rooms begin at $550/night and climb to over $2,000.

Jones Street Guest House
Address: *15 Jones Street*
Telephone: *212-242-1279*
Website: *jonesstreet guesthouse.com*
Subway: *1 to Christopher St.*

This small and intimate option has been around since the late 19th century. The owners live on the 3rd and 4th floor, above the guest apartments.

One option is the Parlor Apartment – the second floor room with wide-plank oak floors overlooking the Village. The other option is the Garden Apartment, which has very low tin ceilings.

The owners also rent out their own duplex, which has a small side yard and working fireplace. They only offer full week stays, for a price of about $1275 and $1400 for the first apartments, which includes a continental breakfast at a nearby café. Plus, you'll feel like you live in an apartment in NYC.

East Village

Until the 1960s, the current space of the East Village was considered part of the Lower East Side. However, with an influx of students, musicians, artists, and hippies, it began to establish its own identity.

Numerous and diverse artistic movements have originated in the East Village, including punk rock and the Nuyorican (New York and Puerto Rican) literary movement.

Eastern Europeans began flooding the neighborhood around 1850. German, Poles, and Ukrainians created a strong community in the neighborhood. Although it has become incredibly gentrified in the past few decades, certain old family-owned eastern European institutions are still in place.

Arts and culture movements of the 1960s and 1970s hit a peak and began to decline as the 1980s rolled around. For a period of time the area was considered unclean and unsafe. However, the streets are now filled with a wealthier young crowd and this area is considered a fun and cool place to be.

See and Do

Tompkins Square Park

L to 1st Avenue

7:00am to dusk daily

500 E 9th Street

Free

nycgovparks.org/parks/tompkins-square-park

Situated in what's known as Alphabet City, this small square has turned from a high-crime area, to a place for East Village residents to spend an afternoon reading or talking over coffee.

A local playground and dog park make it an easy and comfortable place for residents to let their pets and children roam free.

The Tompkins Square Dog Run was the first one in NYC and the park is also noted for its stunning Elm trees.

A number of restaurants and delis line the border making it a great place to grab food and picnic.

Nuyorican Poets Café

 F to 2nd Avenue

 Mon midday to midnight; Tue to Fri midday to 2:00am; Sat 5:00pm to 2:00am; Sun 5:00pm to midnight.

 236 E 3rd Street

 Varies by event.

 nuyorican.org

Since its founding in 1973 in a Rutgers University professor's apartment, this non-profit establishment has grown to be a cultural and literary haven. During big migrations of Puerto Ricans to NYC, there was a demand to establish a Puerto Rican/New York (Nuyorican) identity and place to speak freely.

The venue today has open mic nights, poetry slams, musical performances, and various other events.

The Ukrainian Museum in New York City

 6 to Astor Place

 ukrainianmuseum.org

 Wednesdays to Sundays from 11:30am to 5:00pm

 222 E 6th Street

 Adults: $8, Students and seniors: $6, Children (Under 12): Free

The largest museum in the United States dedicated to Ukrainian cultural Heritage, the institution has been supporting the local community since 1976.

The museum boasts an extensive folk art and fine arts collection, as well as an extensive archive of more than 30,000 items.

KGB Bar

 F to 2nd Avenue

 Event hours vary. See website.

 kgbbar.com

 85 E 4th Street

This Soviet-era themed bar used to be a speakeasy for Ukrainian Socialists who felt compelled to hide during the McCarthyism era.

Now, it's a dive bar/venue for literary readings. Events and readings are usually held nightly.

Neighborhood Guide: East Village

Eat

Abracao
Open: *Tues to Sat 8:00am to 6:00pm; Sun 9:00am to 6:00pm. Closed Mon.*
Address: *81 E 7th Street*
Website: *abraconyc.com*
Subway: *6 to Astor Place*

In operation since 2007, this place is consistently rated one of the best coffee shops in all of NYC, and for good reason. There is also a small, but delicious collection of savory sweets. This place is especially well known for its olive oil cake.

Xi'an's Famous Foods
Open: *Sun to Thurs 11:00am to 11:00pm; Fri & Sat 11:00am to 11:30pm*
Address: *81 St. Mark's Place*
Telephone: *212-786-2068*
Website: *xianfoods.com*
Subway: *6 to Astor Place*

This small NYC Chinese chain began in Flushing, Queens, in 2005. They specialize in the regional cuisine in the area of Xi'an – a region that fuses Chinese and middle eastern flavors.

Menu options include Stewed Pork Hand-Ripped Noodles ($9.50) or Stewed Oxtail Hand-Ripped Noodles in Soup ($12), as well as the smaller options like a Spicy Cumin Lamb Burger ($6). Prices for the authentic quality make it an absolute steal.

Veniero's
Open: *Sun to Thurs 8:00am to midnight; Fri & Sat 8:00am to 1:00am*
Address: *342 E 11th Street*
Telephone: *212-674-7070*

Website: *venierospastry.com*
Subway: *6 to Astor Place; L to 1st Avenue*

Veniero's was started by an Italian immigrant, Anthony Veniero, in 1894. By 1931, he had expanded his menu to a variety of cakes from biscotti, and passed on his family recipes after his death.

This is a New York historical institution, as well as a local favorite for desserts. They have over 200 pastry options to choose from, and they are all delicious. The cannoli, in particular, has a good reputation.

McSorley's Old Ale House
Open: *Mon to Sat 11:00am to 1:00am; Sun 1:00pm to 1:00am*
Address: *15 E 7th Street*
Subway: *6 to Astor Place*

McScorley's is the oldest "Irish" tavern in NYC. In operation since 1854, the pub only began letting women inside after 1970.

Old artwork and newspaper articles cover the walls, and the waiters and staff are what many consider "true Irish." Sawdust covers the floor and the inner décor makes you feel like you could be sitting alongside many of the famous patrons in the past like Abraham Lincoln or Teddy Roosevelt.

There is not a slew of options here; you either get a light or a dark ale, or more typically, one of each. Basic fare is also served.

Momofoku Noodle bar
Open: *Mon to Fri 12:00pm to 4:30pm; Sat & Sun 12:00pm to 4:00pm; Sun to Thur 5:30pm to 11pm; Fri & Sat 5:30pm to 1:00am*
Address: *171 1st Avenue*
Telephone: *212-777-7773*
Website: *momofuku.com/new-york/noodle-bar/*
Subway: *6 to Astor Place; L to 1st Avenue*

This was the first Momofoku restaurant, and has now become a highly regarded institution. The menu changes according to ingredients and seasons but pork buns, ramen noodle bowls, and smaller snacks comprise most of the menu.

They're also known for serving whole fried chicken in southern style and Korean style for reserved parties between 4 and 8 people. Snacks are $2 to $6, small dishes $9 to $16, and large dishes $12 to $18.

Neighborhood Guide: East Village

Stay

The Standard, East Village
Address: *25 Cooper Square*
Telephone: *212-475-5700*
Website: *standard hotels.com/east-village*
Subway: *6 to Astor Place*

This modern chain option has 21 floors with 145 rooms with floor-to-ceiling windows that allow you to marvel at the East Village. Comfortable beds are fitted with Italian sheets and extra large bath towels are provided. Guests can use the gym across the street at Crunch Bowery, and have access to daily newspapers. Rooms begin at $450/night and climb to over $2,000.

The Bowery Hotel
Address: *335 Bowery*
Telephone: *212-505-9100*
Website: *theboweryhotel.com*
Subway: *6 to Bleecker Street*

With 17 stories and 135 rooms and suites, all of the rooms follow a residential

loft design with plenty of natural light and space. Rooms are adorned with hardwood floors and Oushak rugs, along with velvet drapes, 400 Thread Count Egyptian Cotton linens, and marble bathrooms.

Complimentary amenities include bicycles, a film library, newspapers, and WiFi. Pressing, shoe shine, Babysitting, and business services are available on-site. Rooms start at $500/night.

East Village Hotel
Address: *147 1st Avenue*
Telephone: *646-429-9184*
Website: *eastvillagehotel.com*
Subway: *6 to Astor Place; L to 1st Avenue*

This lodging option makes you feel like you are staying less in a hotel and more in a walkup apartment in the neighborhood. Studio style rooms are equipped with a Simmons Beautyrest pillow top bed and with full kitchens. Rooms start at about $350 per night.

SoHo/NoLita

The name SoHo came from the reference to its area "South of Houston Street". NoLita is a newly termed area, short for "North of Little Italy".

Unique to the neighborhood is the cast-iron architecture, the biggest collection in the world. These unique industrial-style buildings were primarily built from 1840 to 1880 with a rise in industrialization.

With growth of the artist population, and a decline in real estate prices, numerous artists moved to SoHo. The industrial lofts with massive windows were an appealing feature for those looking to have studio space in their homes.

In the 1980s, the neighborhood began to fill with more affluent residents and many artists moved to the boroughs. The galleries moved to Chelsea.

Currently, SoHo is known for its endless shopping opportunities. Boutique stores line the narrower streets, as do national and international chains and cafés.

See and Do

New York City Fire Museum

- C/E to Spring Street
- Daily 10:00am to 5:00pm
- 278 Spring Street
- Ad: $8, Stu, Child & Sen: $5
- nycfiremuseum.org

The original New York City Fire Museum opened in Long Island City, Queens in 1934. In 1959 the collection moved to Duane Street in Manhattan. Today it is in a renovated former firehouse built in 1904. This museum takes visitors through the history and evolution of the Fire Department of the City of New York (FDNY).

There is a special memorial to the 343 FDNY members who lost their lives contributing to rescue missions after 9/11.

Leslie-Lohman Museum of Gay and Lesbian Art

 1/2/A/C/E to Canal Street

 leslielohman.org

 Suggested: $9

 Tuesdays to Sundays midday to 6:00pm; Thursdays midday to 8:00pm

 26 Wooster Street

This is the first dedicated LGBTQ art museum in the world. The permanent collection has over 24,000 works of (and about) LGBTQ artists, and showcases various exhibitions throughout the year.

Shopping

SoHo has nearly every store, type, style, etc. available. Roaming the streets and going in and out of stores can provide for entertainment for those interested or curious in fashion. Whether you buy anything or not, it is worth exploring the shops. Some interesting boutiques to check out are Babel Fair, Birchbox, COS, Evolution and Kirna Zabete.

Eat

Balthazar
Open: *Mon to Thur 7:30am to midnight; Fri 7:30am to 1am, Sat 8:00am to 1:00am, Sun 8:00am to midnight.*
Address: *80 Spring Street*
Telephone: *212-965-1785*
Website: *balthazarny.com*
Subway: *6 to Spring Street; N/R to Prince Street*

While you're likely to find their baguettes and other baked items sold throughout NYC, Balthazar also operates a restaurant in the SoHo location. The French bakery serves classic bistro fare for all three meals of the day.

Decadent breakfast options include Eggs Benedict ($23) while a simple Fresh Florida Grapefruit is available too ($11). For lunch or dinner, bistro fare like Sautéed Skate with Savoy cabbage, sherry vinegar sauce, scallions and chives ($35) can be had, as well as grilled Steak au Poivre with spinach and fries ($46).

However, if that is out of your price range, picking up some bread or a pastry is an excellent alternative.

Blue Ribbon Sushi
Open: *Daily midday to 2:00am*
Address: *119 Sullivan Street*
Telephone: *212-343-0404*
Website: *blueribbonrestaurants.com*
Subway: *6 to Spring Street; N/R to Prince Street*

Often considered NYC's best sushi bar, Blue Ribbon Sushi is run by Toshi Ueki. Specials change daily and ingredients are flown in daily from the Pacific Ocean and Sea of Japan.

Rolls go from $6 to $19 and specialty pieces are generally between $4 and $5. Numerous platter options are available and good for sharing.

Café Gitane
Open: *Daily 8:30am to midnight*
Address: *242 Mott Street*
Telephone: *212-334-9552*
Website: *cafegitanenyc.com*
Subway: *N/R to Prince St.*

This quaint Moroccan-style café serves healthy fare and three meals daily. They've made a name for a simple dish – Avocado on seven-grain toast ($7.25) and they serve other combinations atop fresh breads. Salads and specials like Moroccan couscous provide excellent vegetarian options ($15) and meat can always be added for an extra $3.

Alidoro
Open: *Mon to Fri 11:30am to 4:30pm*
Address: *105 Sullivan Street*
Telephone: *212-334-5179*
Website: *alidoronyc.com*
Subway: *C/E to Spring Street*

Alidoro make one thing -

and they make it really well: sandwiches.

It was founded in 1986 in SoHo and they pride themselves on simple but fresh ingredients; they don't Americanize, it's pure Italian. The ingredients are bought fresh from local sources except the meat, which is imported from abroad.

The sandwiches are big and hearty, but can certainly be shared. Most are some combination of prosciutto, mozzarella, roasted peppers, arugula, chicken breast, and eggplant ($10 to $13). Cash only.

Balaboosta
Open: *Tue to Fri 11:30am to 3:30am; Sat to Mon 11:00am to 3:30am*
Address: *214 Mulberry Street*
Telephone: *212-966-7366*
Website: *balaboostanyc.com*
Subway: *N/R to Prince Street*

The name Balaboosta derives from a Yiddish term referring to the perfect housewife. The menu is a new and fresh look at Middle Eastern and Jewish classics prepared with fresh ingredients and care.

Prix Fixe Menus are available for large parties and sharing is typical. Starters like Crispy Cauliflower ($13) and Eggplant Escabeche ($19) are simple but delectable.

The entrées are varied, from Seared Salmon ($27) to the Lamburger ($22) to the Brick Chicken with Israeli couscous, apricots, leeks, and gremolata ($29).

Stay

The Bowery House
Address: *220 Bowery*
Telephone: *212-837-2373*
Website: *theboweryhouse.com*
Subway: *6 to Spring Street; J/Z to Bowery*

This loft-style budget option originally opened in 1927. It was used to lodge soldiers returning home from World War II. Bathrooms were communal and bedrooms made small. The hotel is dedicated to preserving that period, albeit amid cleaner conditions. Rooms, or cabins as they call them, are basic and small and start at about $150/night.

The Broome
Address: *431 Broome Street*
Telephone: *212-431-2929*
Website: *broomestreethotel.com*
Subway: *6 to Spring Street*

Top of the line modern appliances and luxury beds make this hotel a comfortable stay. Complimentary continental breakfasts are served each morning on the patio with fresh, seasonal, and local ingredients. Rooms start at $450/night.

Crosby Street Hotel
Address: *79 Crosby Street*
Telephone: *212-226-6400*
Website: *firmdalehotels.com/hotels/new-york/crosby-street-hotel/*
Subway: *6 to Spring Street; N/R to Prince Street*

Crosby Street is one of the quaintest streets in NYC. The cobblestones and unique boutiques that line the sidewalks make it an idyllic place for a stroll. The hotel has 86 rooms with floor-to-ceiling windows with beautiful views of the city. Rooms are upwards of $1,000 per night.

The Nolitan Hotel
Address: *30 Kenmare Street*
Telephone: *212-925-2555*
Subway: *J/Z to Bowery*

The Nolitan Hotel is described as boutique luxury. The 57 rooms are equipped with plush mattresses. A fitness center offers free classes as well as free bikes and skateboards for guests. A French restaurant is on-site. Rooms average $400 per night.

Lower East Side

The Lower East Side (LES) is an old neighborhood oozing with rich tradition and history.

Ever since immigrants began arriving in New York, the Lower East Side was where people of all different backgrounds – Irish, Italians, Poles, Ukrainians, Germans, and Jews – began forming cultural enclaves and communities.

Gentrification has certainly hit this neighborhood and it has changed.

More Dominicans and Puerto Ricans have moved in, as well as younger upper class adults. However, many of the older rent-stabilized institutions and family businesses have remained in tact.

It is a mixture of the old and new, but it is also one of the few places in NYC where you can really get a sense of what it may have been like years ago.

See and Do

New Museum

F to 2nd Avenue; J/Z to Bowery; 6 to Spring Street

Tue & Wed 11:00am to 6:00pm; Thu 11:00am to 9:00pm; Fri to Sun 11:00am to 6:00pm.

235 Bowery

Ad: $18, Sen: $15, Stu: $12, Child (18 & Under): Free

newmuseum.org

The New Museum was an idea conceived of by Marcia Tucker, who had been working at the Whitney Museum until 1976.

Having been frustrated with the lack of acceptance of artwork by living artists into museums, she set off to start her own.

When she officially founded the institution in 1977, it was the first museum devoted to contemporary art in NYC since World War II.

The seven story, eight-level structure of the building was designed by Japanese architects and is representative of the innovations of the inside work itself.

Thursday evenings from 7:00pm to 9:00pm are 'pay what you wish'. Suggsted minimum of $2.

Neighborhood Guide: Lower East Side

Tenement Museum

J/Z to Bowery

At set times. See website.

103 Orchard Street

Ad: $25, Stu & Sen: $20

tenement.org

The Tenement Museum is an unassuming institution on the Lower East Side that successfully brings the history of immigrants living in NYC between 1869 and 1935 to life.

For those interested in history, this is a prime spot to go, and for those not so interested, this is the place that may spark your curiosity.

The museum is only seen through guided tours. The staff are incredibly well versed, patient, and engaging.

They offer a few different kinds of tours that detail certain aspects of immigrant life, give walking tours of the neighborhood, and have actors that play the roles of the residents of the tenement on Orchard Street. The tours go through tenements and shops that accurately recreate the style of the time. Available with reservation only.

Additionally, the museum has a bookshop with an interesting collection of books about or based in NYC, and various other related trinkets.

Bowery Ballroom

 B/D to Grand Street; F/J/M/Z to Essex/ Delancey Street

 boweryballroom.com

 6 Delancey Street

This music venue in downtown Manhattan was a high-end retail store from the end of World War II until 1998. Now it serves as a music venue for a variety of artists with a capacity of 575 people. Check the website for show and event postings.

Neighborhood Guide: Lower East Side

ABC No Rio

🚇 F/J/M/Z to Delancey/Essex Street

🏠 156 Rivington Street

🌐 abcnorio.org

Founded in 1980, ABC Rio is a collectively run art and activism center.

It has a gallery space, a darkroom, a zine library, a silk-screening studio and a public computer lab.

It is particularly well known for its Punk/Hardcore Collective, which hosts weekly matinees on Saturday afternoon.

Eat

Katz's Delicatessen
Open: *Mon to Wed 8:00am to 10:45pm; Thur 8:00am to 2:45am; opens continuously Fri 8:00am to Sun 10:45pm*
Address: 205 E Houston St
Telephone: 212-254-2246
Website: *katzsdelicatessen.com*
Subway: *F to 2nd Avenue*

Few restaurants can fully capture the quintessential nature of NYC history like Katz's Delicatessen does.

Both tourists and locals frequent this kosher style deli, and it's particularly well known for the iconic sandwich, Pastrami on Rye.

Although the sandwiches may run you up to $20 or $22, they're massive and can be shared.

This is where Meg Ryan filmed the famous scene in 'When Harry Met Sally.'

Originally called Iceland Brothers, the first deli opened in 1888 by two brothers. Willy Katz joined the team in 1903, and Willy's cousin came to help buy out the Iceland brothers in 1910. Finally, in 1917, they moved across the street to the location today.

Always a neighborhood staple, during World War II the owners allowed people to send their sons salami with the slogan, "Send A Salami To Your Boy In The Army."

The deli still uses the old ticket system, where a door attendant hands a printed number ticket to keep track of the tab (a lost ticket fee is $50).

Coming to Katz's is like going to a museum and a restaurant at the same time.

Sons of Essex
Open: *Tues & Wed 5:00pm to midnight; Thurs 5:00pm to 1:00am; Fri 5:00pm to 4:00am; Sat 11:00am to 4:00am; Sun 11:00am to 6:00pm. Closed Mon.*
Address: *133 Essex Street*
Telephone: *212-674-7100*
Website: *sonsofessexnyc.com*
Subway: *J/M/Z to Essex Street; F to Delancey Street*

This restaurant, although emblematic of gentrification, calls on the roots of the past. The menu embodies American comfort food with new age innovations, while creating an atmosphere of Old School Lower East Side in the restaurant.

Fresh salads ($15) and small plates like Truffle Mushroom Pizza ($18) and Lobster & Avocado Toast ($22) are great for sharing.

Russ and Daughters
Open: *Mon to Fri 9:00am to 10:00pm; Sat & Sun 8:00am to 10:00pm*
Address: *179 E Houston Street*
Telephone: *212-475-4880*
Website: *russanddaughters.com*
Subway: *F to 2nd Avenue*

Another long-standing LES classic is Russ & Daughters. Open since 1914, the storefront remains the same, as does the family-style atmosphere.

Joel Russ, a Polish immigrant, grew from selling Polish mushrooms from a Pushcart to selling pickled herrings from this new storefront.

Today, they serve the highest quality fish and caviar in the city. They make good bagels and the go-to combo is a traditional Bagel with Lox and cream cheese.

Mission Chinese Food
Open: *Mon to Sun 5:30pm to 10:45pm, Lunch Sat & Sun only 12:00pm to 4:00pm*
Address: *171 E Broadway*
Website: *missionchinesefood.com*
Subway: *F to East Broadway*

Patrons can order a la carte, or order a varying spread of Chinese delicacies served family style ($69 to $99). Some of the menu options are less typical than you normally see in Chinese restaurant, and have influences of traditional American cuisine, like the beef jerky fried rice.

Stay

Hotel on Rivington
Address: *107 Rivington Street*
Telephone: *212-475-2600*
Website: *hotelonrivington.com*
Subway: *J/M/Z to Essex Street; F to Delancey Street*

Rooms at this LES hotel are spacious, beginning at about 400 square feet each. Many rooms have balconies, soaking tubs, steam showers, and massive glass walls allowing light to flood in. Beds have Tempur-Pedic mattresses, soft linens, and high-end bath amenities. Rooms average about $400 per night.

The Ludlow
Address: *180 Ludlow Street*
Telephone: *212-432-1818*
Website: *ludlowhotel.com*
Subway: *F to 2nd Avenue*

This is a modern and hip lodging option with large windows, comfortable furnishings, and maximum comfort.

Studios, terraces, lofts, are all available online, and a penthouse can be booked upon request. Rooms are between $400 and $550.

Tribeca

While most people know it for the film festival, Tribeca (Triangle Below Canal Street) earned its own neighborhood name in the 1970s.

As the neighborhood struggled significantly following the September 11 attacks, the Tribeca Film Festival was created to promote the recovery.

It has become, in recent years, a very upscale and desirable place to live.

Numerous celebrities reside in Tribeca, and it is often regarded as the safest neighborhood in NYC.

See and Do

The Mysterious Bookshop

 1/2/3 to Chambers Street

 mysteriousbookshop.com

 58 Warren Street

 212-587-1011

This is a bookstore unlike any other. They have a wide selection specializing in mystery novels and periodicals as well as other rare books. The environment and décor make this an enjoyable place to walk around, even if you don't plan on purchasing anything.

The Flea Theater

 N/R to Canal Street; 1 to Franklin Street

 theflea.org

 41 White Street

 212-226-0051

Around since 1996, the Flea Theater was created by three theater artists seeking to create "a joyful hell in a small space." They host and promote off-off Broadway performances, many of which are innovative and experimental. Check the website and calendar for the upcoming productions.

Eat

The Odeon
Open: *Mon & Tue 8:00am to 11:00pm; Wed to Fri 8:00am to midnight; Sat 10:00am to midnight; Sun 10:00am to 11:00pm*
Address: *145 W Broadway*
Telephone: *212-233-0507*
Website: *theodeonrestaurant.com*
Subway: *1/2/3 to Chambers Street*

This classic NYC joint has been around since the 1980s and serves top-quality bistro cuisine in a relaxed environment.

The menu remains simple. For breakfast you may opt for French toast with berries ($17), for lunch a BLT Sandwich on challah ($19) and for dinner a NY Strip Steak with Fries ($40) or Moules Frites ($25).

Sarabeth's
Open: *Mon to Thur 8:00am to 10:30pm; Fri & Sat 8:00am to 11:00pm; Sun 8:00am to 10:00pm*

Neighborhood Guide: Tribeca

Address: *339 Greenwich Street*
Telephone: *212-966-0421*
Website: *sarabethsrestaurants.com*
Subway: *1/2 to Franklin Street*

The Sarabeth's location in Tribeca is famous for their weekend brunch, but the other meal options are also excellent. They have other locations throughout the city and provide high-quality and reliable fare.

For brunch they serve a few different freshly squeezed juices ($8-9) alongside super-sweet options like lemon and ricotta pancakes or pumpkin waffles ($18.50) or famous omelets like Salmon Eggs Benedict ($20.50) which come alongside a pastry.

Stay

Roxy Hotel Tribeca
Address: *2 Avenue of the Americas*
Telephone: *212-519-6600*
Website: *tribecagrand.com*
Subway: *1/2 to Franklin Street*

This luxury option offers 201 guest rooms with high-end fixtures. Included are Egyptian cotton bed and bath linen, Frette bathrobes, and Malin and Goetz bath amenities.

Experienced hotel owners

Tiny's
Open: *Mon to Thur 8:00am to 11:00pm; Fri 8:00am to midnight; Sat 9:00am to midnight; Sun 9:00am to 10:00pm*
Address: *135 W Broadway*
Telephone: *212-374-1135*
Website: *tinysnyc.com*
Subway: *1/2/3 to Chambers Street*

The building in which Tiny's is located dates from 1810, and some of the antiques are over 100 years old. Original tin ceilings, wood paneling, and antique wallpaper make the aesthetic of the place a nice place to enjoy a meal. Starters include items like the kale salad ($17) or house made meatballs ($16).

Entrées include the wild mushroom risotto ($24) as well as a range of freshly prepared meats and fish ($25 to $35).

running the Soho Grand Hotel opened the Tribeca location in 2000, and rapidly experienced high acclaim. Rooms start at $450 per night.

The Frederick Hotel
Address: *95 W Broadway*
Telephone: *212-566-1900*
Website: *cosmohotel.com*
Subway: *1/2/3 to Chambers Street*

The Frederick Hotel (formerly The Cosmopolitan Hotel) is one of the longest

Brandy Library
Open: *Sun to Wed 5:00pm to 1:00am; Thur 4:00pm to 2:00am; Fri & Sat 4:00pm to 4:00am*
Address: *25 N Moore Street*
Telephone: *212-226-5545*
Website: *brandylibrary.com*
Subway: *1/2 to Franklin Street*

If you are into spirits, this is a good place to go. Brandy Library have extended the indoor drinking age to 25 to provide a certain level of maturity in the dimly lit space; they provide rare alcohol, wines, and beers, as well as spirit classes.

They also offer some food options – sandwiches, sushi rolls, and some sides. Whether you're coming for a pre- or post-meal drink, or are here to spend the whole night, this is a nice option.

running hotels in NYC. Constructed in 1838 in a Gothic Revival style, the hotel expanded and was named the Cosmopolitan Hotel in 1869.

It has served some of the most prominent judges, lawyers, and politicians in the past, and continues to do so today. This boutique hotel offers a range of room types with high-end linens and both products. Rooms start at about $325.

Neighborhood Guide: Chinatown

Chinatown

Most cities have a Chinatown of some kind, but Manhattan's Chinatown is home to one of the most densely populated areas in the West, with between 90,000 and 100,000 people.

Chinese immigrants were restricted to migrating to only East Coast cities due to racial discrimination acts of the late 1800s, which is why this area became so highly populated.

When immigration reforms took effect in 1965, a massive influx of Chinese immigrants, specifically from Hong Kong, began coming to New York. Different languages, loyalties, and cultures, led to animosity between some groups. Chinese gangs began forming throughout the Lower East Side and gang warfare was present until the 1990s.

The population continuously moves to other areas of NYC and changes, but the unique grocery stores, restaurants, knock-off brands, and jewelry stores are still prominent in the area.

Many New York natives go there for authentic Chinese fare, or just to experience the busy and intense way of life.

See and Do

Museum of Chinese in America

Since 1980 this museum has been a hub to learn about, preserve, and present information on the history and culture of China. With various displays of history – from multimedia, to oral, to artifact presentation, the curators hope to cultivate a stronger understanding of Chinese-American history.

N/Q to Canal Street

Tue, Wed, Fri, Sat & Sun 11:00am to 6:00pm; Thurs 11:00am to 9:00pm. Closed Mon.

215 Centre Street

Ad: $10, Stu & Sen: $5, Under 12s: Free

mocanyc.org

Free admission for all on the first Thursday of the month.

Eat

Fried Dumpling
Open: *Daily 10:00am to 9:00pm*
Address: *106 Mosco Street*
Telephone: *212-693-1060*
Website: *frieddumplingnyc.com*
Subway: *4/6/J/Z to Canal St.*

Often considered the best dumplings in Chinatown and even more frequently dubbed the best overall value, this is a great option for an almost unbelievably cheap meal.

It is usually $1 for 4 dumplings, and other items are affordably priced too.

Vanessa's Dumpling House
Open: *Mon to Sat 7:30am to 10:30pm, Sun 7:39am to 10:00pm*
Address: *118 Eldrige Street*
Telephone: *212-625-8008*
Website: *vanessas.com*
Subway: *J/M/Z to Essex St.*

Another classic dumpling spot is Vanessa's. Though there are a few other locations in NYC, the one in Chinatown is the best, by a significant margin. Dumplings can be had on a plate or in soup; usually 8 are in an order for $4. Also available are sesame pancake sandwiches ($1 to $3), soups and noodle dishes.

Joe's Shanghai
Open: *Daily 11:00am to 11:00pm*
Address: *9 Pell Street*
Telephone: *212-233-8888*
Website: *joeshanghairestaurants.com*
Subway: *J/Z/N/Q to Canal Street; B/D to Grand Street*

Founded in Queens, Joe's Shanghai has been in NYC since 1995. They've become famous for their soup dumplings, which are handcrafted and made to order. They come to the table in hot bamboo steamers in a light broth. One order is about $8.

Vivi Bubble Tea
Open: *Sun to Thur 10:00am to 10:00pm; Fri & Sat 10:00am to 10:30pm*
Address: *49 Bayard Street*
Telephone: *212-566-6833*
Website: *vivibubbletea.com*
Subway: *J/Z/N/Q to Canal Street*

This Taiwanese tea-based drink has become a hit in NYC in recent years. The popular drink consists of a thick drink with fruit or milk and the signature tapioca balls, which can be slurped through the oversized plastic straws.

Vivi's opened in 2007 and has been offering the classics, as well as innovative teas, to both Asian customers and others.

From the Japanese Matcha to Cappuccino Milk tea, there is a wide variety of options that cater to range of palates.

Little Italy

Although Little Italy has gotten progressively smaller over the years, its presence can certainly be felt. Since the original immigrants arrived and established businesses, there has been a slow and gradual decline of Italian presence.

The major influx and expansion of Chinatown, as well as the expansion of the Lower East Side, have contributed to Little Italy's shrinking influence.

All that said, there are still a few blocks worth roaming that will give you the sense of what the more robust Little Italy was like not too long ago. Restaurant owners will greet you on the sidewalk and urge you to come and try their food.

The 11-day street fair in September of San Gennaro on Mulberry Street is a reminder of the legacy that Italian-Americans have had on NYC.

Eat

La Mela
Open: *11:30am to 2:00am*
Address: *167 Mulberry Street*
Telephone: *212-431-9493*
Website: *lamelarestaurant.com*
Subway: *J/Z to Bowery*

This classic Italian joint provides a festive and fun dinner option. Family-style menus are available from $28 per person. They'll bring an appetizer of fresh mozzarella and tomatoes, followed by hot antipasti and a range of pastas.

No matter how hungry you are, there is more than enough options to fill you up. The place provides a homey environment with red and white-checkered tablecloths. It is a fun place to spend an evening.

Rubirosa
Open: *Sun to Wed 11:30am to 11:00pm, Thur to Sat 11:30am to midnight.*
Address: *235 Mulberry St.*
Telephone: *212-965-0500*
Website: *rubirosanyc.com*
Subway: *6 to Spring Street*

This restaurant opened after Joe and Pat's Pizzeria on Staten Island gained high recognition selling thin-crust pizza. They sell pastas and meat, but most people come for the delicious pizza.

With options aside from the classic tomato and mozzarella, you can order a vodka pizza, sausage and broccoli rabe pizza, or an arugula pizza with various cheese, vegetable, and meat add-ons ($18 to $30).

Ferrara Bakery
Open: *Sun to Thurs 9:00am to 11:00pm; Fri & Sat 9:00am to midnight*
Address: *195 Grand Street*
Telephone: *212-226-6150*
Website: *ferraranyc.com*
Subway: *J/Z to Bowery*

This old Italian family bakery has its origins three generations back in 1892. It was a place where Italians would gather late at night after an opera, play some card games, drink espresso, and have some cannoli. Other classic Italian desserts are available – napoleons, eclairs, and pasticcios, along with an array of gelato flavors.

Financial District

The Financial District was where the interaction between colonizers and the original Native Americans that lived in present day Manhattan began. Now, it is the area of major financial institutions' headquarters.

The New York Stock Exchange and the Federal Reserve Bank of New York are located on the southern tip of Manhattan, along with most NYC government offices.

The residential population has nearly doubled in size since the turn of the century, and it continues to grow.

The narrow cobblestone streets are reminders of the old New York and the modern glass skyscrapers are emblematic of the present day clientele. It's a wondrous place to wander around and marvel at how fast the whole city has developed.

See and Do

Museum of American Finance

 2/3 to Wall Street

 moaf.org

 Tuesdays to Saturdays 10:00am to 4:00pm

 48 Wall Street

 Adults: $8, Students and seniors: $5, Children (Under 6): Free

This institution prides itself on being the only public museum focused on preserving, teaching, and displaying the history and importance of American finance. Permanent exhibitions explain the basics regarding financial markets, money, banking, and entrepreneurship.

National Museum of the American Indian – New York

 4/5 to Bowling Green

 nmai.si.edu

 Free

 Daily from 10:00am to 5:00pm, with late closing at 8:00pm on Thurs

 1 Bowling Green

Affiliated with the larger museum in Washington D.C., this Smithsonian Institution has exhibitions exploring the diversity of Native American people in the United States. The combination between permanent and temporary exhibitions provides everyone something to offer.

9/11 Memorial, Museum & One World Observatory

 A/C to Chambers St. or Fulton St.; E to World Trade Center; 1/2/3 to Chamber Streets; R to Cortlandt Street; 1/R to Rector Street

 180 Greenwich Street

 911memorial.org

The events of September 11, 2001, greatly changed NYC, and its residents have not forgotten it. In 2011, this memorial opened.

Michael Arad and Peter Walker's design, "Reflecting Absence" was chosen and construction began in 2006. The memorial consists of two one-acre pools with the largest man-made waterfalls in the United States.

The victims' names are inscribed on bronze plates that are attached to the walls of the pools. Other trees fill the rest of the 6 acre plaza.

In 2014, the museum opened to the public. The exhibits have numerous images, artifacts, and oral histories of the people who lost their lives. In our opinion, it is the best museum in the city.

Finally, also located on-site is One World Trade Center, the tallest building in the US. At 1,776 feet tall, this building dominates NYC's skyline. On floors 100 to 102 you can visit the One World Observatory viewing deck.

Pricing and Hours:
Memorial – *Open: Daily from 7:30am to 9:00pm.*

Free Admission.

Museum – *Open: Sun to Thurs 9:00am to 8:00pm; Fri & Sat 9:00am to 9:00pm. Free Admission: Tuesdays after 5:00pm. Other Days: Adults: $24, Seniors, Students: $20, Veterans: $18, Ages 7 to 17: $15, Child Age 6 and under: Free. Last admission 2 hours before closing.*

One World Observatory – *Open: Daily 9:00am to 9:00pm - early opening from 8:00am May to August. Adults: $34, Seniors $32 and Children $28.*

South Street Seaport

🚇 2/3 to Fulton Street

🏠 Fulton Street

🌐 southstreetseaport.com

This historic area on the East River has been used as a significant port since the mid 1600s.

Today, the South Street Seaport Museum can be viewed to learn about the history of the Seaport's importance.

With stores, places to eat, and opportunities to learn about the history, the South Street Seaport is an easy place to spend an entire morning or afternoon.

Bowling Green Park

🚇 4/5 to Bowling Green

🏠 Whitehall Street

🌐 nycgovparks.org/parks/bowling-green

Bowling Green is NYC's oldest park with a rich history. It is next to the site of the original Dutch fort of New Amsterdam and the original 18th century fence is still standing, which surrounds the park.

The park is well known for the bronze "Charging Bull" sculpture, which symbolizes intense financial optimism and prosperity. It was brought to the park in 1989 by guerilla artist Arturo Di Modica.

Neighborhood Guide: Financial District

Statue of Liberty and Ellis Island

 1 to South Ferry; 4/5 to Bowling Green

 Winter: 9:30am to 3:30pm. Summer: 8:30am to 5:00pm.

 1 Battery Place

 Ad: $18.50, Ages 4 to 12: $9, Sen: $4. Add $3 for crown.

 statuecruises.com

Perhaps the most famous symbol of New York City, the Statue of Liberty is a must on any NY itinerary.

The only way to visit the Statue of Liberty is on a cruise run by Statue Cruises. Ferries depart from Battery Park in New York and Liberty State Park in New Jersey.

Once aboard the fery you will travel to Ellis Island and learn about the Immigration experience of many arriving to the city in hope of a new life. The audio guide is truly fascinating and haunting at the same time.

Next, take a ferry to Liberty Island and learn about the Statue of Liberty with the included audio guide.

To visit the Statue's pedestal, you must reserve in advance. You can then also climb over 400 steps to reach the crown of the Statue of Liberty (advance reservation also required).

Complimentary guided park ranger tours are available.

Museum of Jewish Heritage

 1 to Rector Street; 4/5 to Bowling Green

 mjhnyc.org

 Sun, Mon & Tue 10:00am to 6:00pm, Wed & Thur 10:00am to 8:00pm, Fri 10:00am to 5:00pm, Closed Sat

 36 Battery Place

 Adults: $12, Seniors: $10, Students: $7, Under 12s: Free

This museum seeks to educate people about Jewish life before, during, and after the holocaust.

Exhibitions and collections are displayed year round to hone in on particular stories that are representative of Jewish culture.

All visitors will go through the entry rotunda and view a nine-minute multimedia presentation about the themes of the museum.

Then, you move on to peruse through parts of the 25,000-piece permanent collection as well as temporary exhibitions.

Free admission for all on Wednesdays and Thursdays from 4:00pm to 8:00pm

Neighborhood Guide: Financial District

Eat

Delmonicos
Open: *Mon to Fri 11:30am to 10:00pm; Sat 5:00pm to 10:00pm. Closed sun.*
Address: *56 Beaver Street*
Telephone: *212-509-1144*
Website: *delmonicosrestaurant.com*
Subway: *J/Z to Broad Street; 2/3 to Wall Street*

Delmonico's began serving New Yorkers in 1827, selling pastries, coffee, wines, and liquors out of a small shop. In the location it stands now, the family opened the first fine dining restaurant in the United States in 1837.

Now, it stands as a classic Steak house selling crab cakes ($24), crispy oysters ($22), double cut lamb chops ($49), and a variety of steaks.

The Dead Rabbit Grocery and Grog
Open: *11:00am to 4:00pm*
Address: *30 Water Street*
Telephone: *626-422-7906*
Website: *deadrabbitnyc.com*
Subway: *N/R to Whitehall Street*

This two-floor establishment offers both a place to enjoy a craft beer or cocktail, as well as enjoy a satisfying meal. It has won awards like the Best American Cocktail Bar in 2014, and one of the world's 50 best bars in 2013 and 2014.

Vintage cocktails are done seasonally, and are shaken, not stirred. They have clever names like "Talk of the devil" and "Ace of Spades"($18).

Stay

Gild Hall
Address: *15 Gold Street*
Telephone: *212-232-7700*
Website: *thompsonhotels.com/hotels/gild-hall*
Subway: *2/3 to Fulton Street*

This luxury hotel option has rooms filled with leather indicative of designer Jim Walrod's vision of creating a country house-like feel. Regular rooms are between $400-$560 and the luxury suites go up to $1,500.

Residence Inn
Address: *170 Broadway*
Telephone: *212-600-8900*
Website: *marriott.com/hotels/travel/nycrl-residence-inn-new-york-manhattan-world-trade-center-area/*
Subway: *4/5 to Fulton Street*

This hotel offers a range of comfortable rooms in the heart of the financial district. A fitness room and complimentary breakfast are available on site. Prices begin at $350 and go up to about $650.

Andaz Wall Street
Address: *75 Wall Street*
Telephone: *212-590-1234*
Website: *wallstreet.andaz.hyatt.com*
Subway: *2/3 to Wall Street*

These loft-style guest rooms are situated just a short walk from the East River and rooms have a complimentary mini-bar.

The rooms are more spacious than the average New York City room – 11-foot-high ceilings and 345-square-foot rooms. Walk-in showers and Beekman bath products are included as well. Rooms start from about $550 per night.

The Wall Street Inn
Address: *9 S William Street*
Telephone: *877-747-1500*
Website: *thewallstreetinn.com*
Subway: *4/5 to Bowling Green*

This newly renovated building is set atop the lower Manhattan cobblestone streets and one of the oldest streets in Manhattan. After a series of ownerships and fires, the current address was bought in the 1990s by Holocaust survivors and opened in 1999.

The rooms have marble tile baths, full-length mirrors, and are spacious. They are decorated with a classy style. Rooms cost between $350 and $450 per night.

Neighborhood Guide: Brooklyn

Brooklyn

Brooklyn has roots in some of the earliest battles in the Revolutionary War. George Washington tread over places like the Grand Army Plaza and Atlantic Avenue in order to push back some of the British troops.

The village of Brooklyn was established in 1816. At the time, people went back and forth between Manhattan on a ferry to Wall Street, to what is now Brooklyn Heights. For much of the 19th century, Brooklyn was considered to be a twin city of New York, geographically bigger than Manhattan, and highly populated.

When the Brooklyn Bridge was completed in 1883, the city merged with Manhattan to become NYC. The Brooklyn Navy Yard was an instrumental facility throughout World War II, and employed 70,000 people at its peak. Now there is a big mix of Brooklynites working in Brooklyn and Manhattan.

When people think of NYC, they generally think of the picturesque Manhattan – the skyline defined by the Empire State Building, Times Square, etc.

Even ten years ago, Brooklyn was a place tourists wouldn't visit, yet it also was a place Manhattanites avoided. However, in recent years, the borough has began to define itself as a separate entity with a lot to offer.

While population density may be associated with Manhattan, Brooklyn is the most populated borough in NYC with over 2.5 million people. And the diverse population brings a lot of flavor to the city.

The amount of time you have to spend in NYC will naturally affect how much of the outer boroughs you see, but if you have some time, exploring Brooklyn is worthwhile.

See and Do

Barclay's Center

| | 2/3/4/5/B/D/N/Q/R to Atlantic Avenue – Barclays Center | barclayscenter.com | 620 Atlantic Avenue |

This multi-purpose indoor arena was deliberated over the course of many years but finally opened to the public in September of 2012. It is the home of the Brooklyn Nets basketball team, the hockey team, and the New York Islanders.

The design is modern and industrial, and from the exterior has a glass curtain wall with steel panels, intended to bring about the history and look of Brooklyn's brownstone apartments.

Various concerts and sporting events occur throughout the year.

Williamsburg

This neighborhood is one of the epicenters of hipster culture and embodies gentrification.

It has been home to many ethnic enclaves, and two in particular still maintain a presence – orthodox Jews and Puerto Ricans.

In the northern part of Williamsburg and eastwards there are mostly young white people, which has led to a lot of high-end vintage stores, unique eateries, and galleries opening up.

Subway: L to Bedford Avenue

Prospect Park

Like Central Park, Prospect Park was designed by Frederick Law Olmsted. Although smaller in size, many argue Prospect Park is NYC's nicest public park.

Within the boundaries is the Prospect Park Zoo, a nature conservancy, a boathouse, and the Prospect Park Bandshell which hosts many free concerts during the summer.

Even as the weather gets nice and people in NYC flock to public parks, Prospect Park

retains the intimacy and solitude that Central Park often lacks during beautiful weather.

Brooklyn Bridge

 4/5/6 to Brooklyn Bridge; N/R City Hall; A/C High Street; F York Street

 bit.ly/brookbrid

The Brooklyn Bridge is one of the most iconic sites to see in all of New York City. The Brooklyn Bridge is a unique fixture not just in New York, but also in the world.

The hybrid cable-stayed/ suspension bridge was completed in 1883 and connects lower Manhattan to Dumbo and Brooklyn Heights.

The bridge itself is an architectural masterpiece, and unlike the two other bridges that connect Manhattan to Brooklyn – the Manhattan and the Williamsburg bridges – a subway line does not run across it.

Walking from Manhattan to Brooklyn, you can make your way to Brooklyn Bridge Park, which provides spectacular views of Manhattan at sunset.

The bridge is 1.1 mi/1.8 km in length and is open 24/7.

Coney Island

Between 1880 and World War II, Coney Island was the largest amusement area in the United States and attracted millions of people each year. There were three amusement parks, and the area became a resort destination for many. However, two main amusement parks faltered, but there was a resurgence in the 1970s.

Luna Park is now in operation today. There are newer rides but three main attractions are historical icons. The Wonder Wheel, a Ferris wheel built in 1918 holds 144 riders and still spins today. The Parachute Jump debuted at the 1939 World's Fair does not operate but can be viewed. And finally, the iconic roller coaster, The Cyclone, built in 1927 stands as the United States' oldest wooden roller coaster; it is still in operation today.

The other historical and iconic structure at Coney Island is the original site of Nathan's Hot Dogs. It is also the site where Nathan's Hot Dog Eating Contest has been held since 1972.

Coney Island is no longer considered the resort destination it was built to be, especially with a large majority of the residents living in public housing. But if you have time, historically and culturally, it is a fascinating part of NYC.

Subway: D/F/N/Q to Coney Island – Stillwell Avenue

Brooklyn Museum

	2/3 to Eastern Parkway		brooklynmuseum.org
	Wed, Fri, Sat, Sun 11:00am to 6:00pm; Thu 11:00am to 10:00pm. Closed Mon & Tues.		200 Eastern Parkway
	Adults: $16, Students and seniors: $10, Children (19 and Under): Free		

With 1.5 million works in a space of 560,000 square feet, the Brooklyn Museum is NYC's second largest in size.

There are substantial collections in the Egyptian Antiquities, as well as African, Oceanic, and Japanese art. Popular American artists represented are Mark Rothko, Georgia O'Keefe, Norman Rockwell, Edgar Degas, and others.

Interesting temporary exhibits change year round.

There is free admission on the first Saturday of the month.

Eat

Roberta's
Open: *Mon to Fri 11:00am to midnight; Sat & Sun 10:00am to midnight*
Address: *261 Moore Street*
Telephone: *718-417-1118*
Website: *robertaspizza.com*
Subway: *L to Morgan Av*

Situated in the warehouse, loft-apartment style neighborhood of Bushwick, many argue that this is one of the best pizza restaurants in all of NYC.

The Neapolitan-style pizza is made in a wood-burning oven with airy and crispy crust and fresh sauces and cheeses.

You can order the simple originals ($13 to $16) or be a bit more daring and go for something like the Beatmaster – a pizza with tomato, mozzarella, gorgonzola, pork sausage, onions, capers, and jalapenos ($19).

Torst
Open: *Sun to Wed midday to midnight; Thursdays midday to 2:00am; Fri & Sat midday to 3:00am*
Address: *615 Manhattan Av*
Telephone: *718-389-6034*
Website: *torstnyc.com*
Subway: *G to Nassau Av*

For those into beer, few better places can be found than Torst, a beer bar that receives high acclaim.

On the border of Williamsburg and Greenpoint, the Danish-style bar has Scandinavian chairs from the 1950s, and a high-tech glass-enclosed control panel under the taps so the bar stewards can calibrate the nitrogen and carbon dioxide mixes to make the compression perfect.

They have 21 beers on tap, which change regularly, and have over 200 beers by the bottle.

They also serve fresh-baked bread, cheese and meat plates, and a few sandwiches ($10 to $16).

Junior's
Open: *Sun to Thur 6:30am to midnight; Fri & Sat 6:30am to 1:00am*
Address: *386 Flatbush Avenue Extension*
Telephone: *718-852-5257*
Website: *juniorscheesecake.com*

If you're walking through downtown Brooklyn, Junior's is a tough place to miss. There are a few other locations too – in Grand Central, Times Square, and in Connecticut.

Harry Rosen worked with a baker to create "The World's Most Fabulous Cheesecake" based on a family recipe. In 1950, he opened Junior's. They serve soups, salads, sandwiches, and more, but they're most well known for their desserts.

Diner
Open: *Mon to Thur 6:00pm to midnight, Fri 11:00am to 5:00pm, 6:00pm to midnight; Sat & Sun 10:00am to midnight*
Address: *85 Broadway*
Telephone: *718-486-3077*
Website: *dinernyc.com*
Subway: *J/M/Z to Marcy Av*

Opening in 1999 in a Kullman train car underneath the Williamsburg Bridge, Diner is emblematic of the old-new feelings of the area.

The menus change daily and use only fresh ingredients. Items in the past have included pork croquettes over creamy grits with fried eggs, watercress, and salsa, and a beef burger ($15).

Buttermilk Channel
Open: *Mon to Thur 11:30am to 3:00pm and 5:00pm and 10:00pm, Fri 11:30am to 3:00pm and 5:00pm to 11:30pm, Sat 10:00am to 3:00pm and 5:00pm to 11:30pm, Sun 10:00am to 3:00pm and 5:00pm to 10:00pm*
Address: *524 Court Street*
Telephone: *718-852-8490*
Website: *buttermilkchannelnyc.com*
Subway: *F/G to Smith Street*

Buttermilk Channel is named after the strait between Brooklyn and Governors Island. Doug Crowell, the owner and the graduate of the Culinary Institute of America, and Chefs Ryan Angulo and Jon Check have crafted menus that bring new flavors to more traditional bistro and American fare.

Queens

Like Brooklyn, Queens was its own city and county until its incorporation to NYC as a borough in 1807. During the American Revolution, Queens remained relatively untouched. When the Queensboro Bridge was finished in 1909, transportation between Queens and Manhattan became more accessible, and more people began commuting between the two boroughs.

In 1939, Queens was the site of the New York Word's Fair and LaGuardia Airport opened. JFK Airport opened in 1948 and Queens again hosted the New York World's Fair in 1964, bringing more and more visitors to the borough.

Today, Queens is the most ethnically diverse urban area in the world.

See and Do

Astoria

For most of the 19th and early 20th century, Astoria saw an influx of Irish, Italian, and Jewish immigrants into the neighborhood.

When the 1960s rolled around, a large number of Greeks and immigrants from Cyprus came into the area, opening up restaurants and bakeries that exist today.

In more recent years, the Arab population has been growing. Thus, on every street corner there are new odors to smell, new foods to taste, and different people to talk to.

Subway: N/Q to Broadway

Museum of the Moving Image

 M/R to Steinway Street

 movingimage.us

 Wed & Thu 10:30am to 5:00pm; Fri 10:30am to 8:00pm; Sat & Sun 10:30am to 6:00pm

 36-01 35th Avenue

 Adults: $15, Students and seniors: $11, Ages 3 to 17: $9, Under 3s: Free. Free admission Fridays between 4:00pm and 8:00pm.

This museum is the only in the United States that is dedicated to all aspects of moving images. From the art, history, technique, and technology, exhibits encompass a wide range of subjects and the collection is unique and for people of all ages.

Flushing

While Manhattan certainly boasts a noteworthy Chinatown, the Chinese-immigrant population of Flushing, Queens, is far denser, insular, and more robust. This is a place to go to get a real taste for what its like to live in an Asian city. You'll find authentic cuisine, rare Japanese animé editions, and much more.

Subway: 7 to Flushing – Main Street

Socrates Sculpture Park

N/Q to Broadway

Daily 10:00am to sunset

32-01 Vernon Boulevard

Free

socrates sculpturepark.org

Socrates Sculpture Park is situated on land that was an abandoned landfill and illegal dumpsite. It was founded in 1986, as the first space dedicated to exhibiting large-scale sculptures. The park is right on the East River and on a nice day is a great place for a picnic.

The Noguchi Museum

N/Q to Canal Street

Wed to Fri 10:00am to 5:00pm; Sat & Sun 11:00am to 6:00pm. Closed Mon & Tues.

9-01 33rd Road

Ad: $10, Stud & Sen: $5, Child (Under 12): Free

noguchi.org

Based on a Japanese-American artist, Isamu Noguchi, this museum is situated in an old industrial building with an open-air sculpture garden and reflective space to contemplate the works.

The collection exhibits a range of sculptures, portraits, drawings, designs, lunar projects, and more.

On the first Friday of every month, admission is free.

Flushing Meadows – Corona Park

The fourth biggest public park in NYC, Flushing Meadows contains the USTA Billie Jean King National Tennis Center, The Met's Citi Field, the New York Hall of Science, the Queens Museum of Art, the Queens Wildlife Center, and other features.

It was also the location of the 1939 and 1964 World's Fair, and the enormous sculptural Unispheres can still be viewed in the park.

On weekends families will bring barbecue food, soccer/footballs, and other games to spend the day.

Subway: 7 to 111 Street

MoMA PS1

If you're interested in experimental art, there is no better place to go than MoMA PS1. One of the oldest and largest non-profit contemporary art institutions in the United States, the art exhibited at MoMA PS1 will challenge your notions of what it means for something to be art.

 E/M to Court Sqaure-23rd Street; 7 to Court Square

 momaps1.org

 Thur to Mon midday to 6:00pm, closed Tues & Wed

 22-25 Jackson Avenue

 Adults: $10, Students and seniors: $5, Children (Under 16): Free

Eat

Taverna Kyclades
Open: *Mon to Thurs midday to 11:00pm; Fri & Sat midday to 11:30pm; Sun midday to 10:30pm*
Address: *33-07 Ditmars Blvd*
Telephone: *718-545-8666*
Website: *tavernakyclades.com*
Subway: *N/Q to Astoria – Ditmars Boulevard*

If you do find yourself in Astoria and get a craving for some Greek food, most restaurants in the area are good bets. However, Taverna Kyclades has a reputation that exceeds many others.

Classic Greek staples like stuffed grape leaves ($6.75) or spinach pie ($7.50) can be shared as appetizers.

For entrées, many opt for the meats, like a Chicken Kebab with lemon potatoes ($14.50) or fresh grilled fish.

New World Mall Food Court
Open: *Daily 9:00am to 10:00pm*
Address: *136-20 Roosevelt Avenue*
Telephone: *718-353-0551*
Website: *newworldmallny.com*
Subway: *7 to Flushing – Main Street*

The mall – the largest indoor Asian Market in the State of New York has 108 retail shops, an enormous Asian Supermarket, and a food cart serving 32 different Asian foods from throughout the continent.

Bright lights, a hectic atmosphere, and foods and smells that look entirely unfamiliar to most fill the mall, providing a truly unique cultural experience.

Mustang Thakali Kitchen
Open: *Mon to Thur 11:00am to 11:00pm; Fri 11:30am to 11:30pm, Sat & Sun midday to midnight*
Address: *74-14 37th Avenue*
Telephone: *718-898-5088*
Subway: *E/F/M/R to Jackson Heights – Roosevelt; 7 to 74th Street – Broadway*

Jackson Heights is one of the most diverse neighborhoods in NYC and has dense enclaves of South Americans, as well as South and East Asians. Naturally, numerous good and authentic ethnic eateries are available. One such restaurant is Mustang Thakali Kitchen. With an unassuming storefront, this establishment has made a name for its delicious Nepalese delicacies.

Most entrées come with a clump of rice in the middle surrounded by a combination of different stews. The popular yogurt-based lassi drinks offset some of the spices.

Neighborhood Guide: The Bronx

The Bronx

Named after the Bronx River, the Bronx was originally part of Westchester County until the latter part of the 19th century. When the City of New York was established in 1898, the Bronx became a borough. In the beginning of the 20th century, the area was a manufacturing hub. In 1919 the Bronx had 63 piano factories alone.

The Bronx's population grew rapidly, along with the manufacturing industry, until the 1950s. After World War I, residential construction increased and Irish, Italian, and Jewish Americans began settling in the area.

However, after World War II and the Great Depression, the borough began an economic decline and an increase in crime and poverty.

Since the 1980s, revitalization and development has begun to take place in the borough and the Bronx is seen to be on a continuous rise.

Even though one fifth of the area of the Bronx is made up by parkland, it is still the third most densely populated county in the United States.

It's known for being the "Birthplace of Hip Hop" and the home of Yankee fans.

See and Do

The Edgar Allan Poe Cottage

For those interested in literary history, the Edgar Allan Poe Museum may be an interesting day trip. Opened in 1922, this old stone house is just a few blocks away from the notoriously dark writer's first Richmond home. The museum has a collection of Poe's manuscripts, letters, first editions, and other belongings.

B/D to Kingsbridge Road

Thur & Fri 10:00pm to 3:00pm, Sat 10:00am to 4:00pm, Sun 1:00pm to 5:00pm

1914-16 East Main Street

Ad: $8, Stu & Sen: $6

poemuseum.org

Bronx Zoo

 2/5 to Bronx Park East

 Mon to Fri 10:00am to 5:00pm; Sat & Sun 10:00am to 5:30pm

 2300 Southern Boulevard

 Ad: $37, Sen: $32, Child: $27, Under 2s: Free

 bronxzoo.com

This 265-acre facility of wildlife and habitats is the perfect urban escape, especially for those with kids. Popular exhibits like Tiger Mountain, Himalayan Highlands, Congo Gorilla Forest, and the World of Reptiles are geared towards entertaining all ages. There are also a carousel, a 4D theatre and seasonal camel rides, a monorail and a shuttle.

Bronx Brewery

 6 to Cypress Avenue

 thebronxbrewery.com

 718-402-1000

 856 E 136th Street

 Change seasonally. Open daily in the afternoon; hours from between 12:00pm to 8:00pm and 3:00pm to 7:00pm. Check website to confirm.

Most people go to the Brooklyn Brewery if they're planning on visiting a Brewery in NYC. However, the Tasting Room and outdoor Backyard make the Bronx Brewery a tough competitor.

You can visit the brewery, do tastings, and carry out some pints.

Since the official launch in 2011, the brewery has grown rapidly and increased its distribution.

Botanical Gardens

 B/D to Kingsbridge Road

 nybg.org

 Tuesdays to Sundays 10:00am to 6:00pm

 2900 Southern Boulevard

 Weekdays – Adults: $23, Students & seniors: $20, Under 12s: $10, Under 2s: Free; Weekends – Adults: $28, Students & seniors: $25, Under 12s: $12, Under 2s: Free

Since its founding in 1891, the Botanical Garden has been the perfect oasis outside of the NYC metropolis.

There are 250 acres to browse through with plants and flora that exist in a variety of climates.

You'll be able to smell the odors and see the textures of tropical, desert, and temperate botany.

Eat

Enzo's Italian Restaurant
Address: *1998 Williamsbridge Road*
Hours: *Tues to Sat 12:00pm to 10:00pm, Sun 1:00pm to 9:00pm, closed Mon.*
Telephone: *718-409-3828*
Website: *enzosbronxrestaurant.com*
Subway: *5 to Morris Park*

Although some think of Manhattan when they hear about Little Italy, other New Yorkers think of Arthur Avenue in the Bronx.

Generations of Italian families in the area have kept businesses and restaurants with traditional Italian fare. Enzo's is one of the best.

The food is traditional, Eggplant Rollatini ($11), Bistecca Milanese ($26), and Penne alla Vodka ($18), and made with the freshest ingredients.

188 Bakery Chuchifritos
Address: *158 E 188th Street*
Hours: *Daily 9:00am to midnight*
Telephone: *718-367-4500*
Subway: *B/D to Fordham Road*

This Puerto Rican diner makes some of the best Mofongo – a dish of fried plantains decorated with meats and other stews. Typical toppings include cheese, pork chops, or chicharrones ($8). Other Puerto Rican beloved staples bring together numerous locals of both Puerto Rican descent and otherwise.

The Good Dine
Address: *3922 White Plains Road*
Hours: *s*
Telephone: *718-325-3463*
Subway: *2/5 to 219th Street*

Said to be the Bronx's best Jamaican restaurant (and one of many) is The Good Dine. The plate of Oxtail is particularly well-renowned ($7 to $12). Other combinations of rice, beans, and meats often are cooked with fiery spices.

The storefront of this unassuming dining spot should not deter you; the take out food containers contain some of the best Caribbean food in the whole city. Be aware that the staff are not known for their customer service.

Staten Island

Often the most neglected and forgotten borough is Staten Island. Even prior to colonization, the tribe that inhabited the land of Staten Island was a separate division of the larger Lenape people. The island later became an important territory during the Revolutionary War, as the British took control of the land.

In 1776, 140 British ships arrived on Staten Island to launch an invasion of New York. The Battle of Staten Island occurred in 1777 with inconclusive outcomes and the British inhabited the island until their final evacuation in 1783.

As with the rest of the boroughs, the towns of Staten Island disappeared and it became a borough in 1898.

The Verrazano-Narrows Bridge was completed in 1964 and connected Staten Island to New Jersey, and Brooklyn. This led to a significant population growth on the Island throughout the next few decades.

Staten Island is known for its natural habitats. Fresh Kills, a freshwater estuary, and other wetlands have been designated a Significant Coastal Fish and Wildlife Habitat. The Freshkills Park was a project implemented after 9/11, which is being built over public landfill.

Significant Italian, Russian, Polish, and Sri Lankan communities reside throughout the Island, as do a few other ethnic groups.

See and Do

Historic Richmond Town

 Oakwood Heights

 historicrichmondtown.org

 Wednesdays to Sundays 1:00pm to 5:00pm. Closed Mondays & Tuesdays

 441 Clarke Avenue

 Adults: $8, Students and seniors: $6, Children (4 to 11): $5

This preserved historic town and farm with artifacts and structures from the 17th century sits in the middle of the island. For two centuries Richmond was the government center of Staten Island, known as Richmond County until 1898.

This old preserved area is an odd glimpse into what life was like over one hundred years ago. Guided tours are at 1:30pm Wednesday to Friday, and at 1:00pm and 3:00pm on Saturday and Sunday.

The Staten Island Ferry

1 to South Ferry

Every 15 to 30 minutes, runs 24 hours per day

4 Whitehall Street

Free

siferry.com

The Staten Island Ferry is not only the most convenient way to get from Manhattan to the island, but it is also an event in and of itself. The views of Manhattan, the Statue of Liberty, and Ellis Island are particularly magnificent. If you can time it so you're riding the Ferry at sunset, prepare yourself for an idyllic setting.

Freshkills Park

With 2,200 acres, Freshkills Park is nearly three times the size of Central Park.

In 2001 the planning began to create a massive green space over a former landfill. Though the park is not fully complete (and won't be until the 2030s), much of it is up and running and there are many opportunities for outdoor recreation.

Website: freshkillspark.org

Sailor's Snug Harbor

 1000 Richmond Terrace   snug-harbor.org

This area was founded to be a relaxation spot for retired sailors in 1801. All in all, this area consists of 26 historic buildings, nine botanical gardens, a two-acre urban farm, and 10 acres of wetlands.

It is a place where a variety of culture is presented and comes together. From architecture to visual art, to theater, to dance, to music, to environmental science, a lot can be found.

Exhibitions and performances change throughout the year. Hours and admissions vary depending on the sites.

Eat

Denino's Pizzeria and Tavern
Open: *Sun to Thur 11:00am to 11:00pm; Fri & Sat 11:00am to midnight*
Address: *524 Port Richmond Avenue*
Telephone: *718-442-9401*
Website: *deninos.com*

This family owned establishment opened as a Tavern shortly after the repeal of Prohibition in 1937. In 1951, they began serving pizza and by the 1990s began gaining critical acclaim for serving the best pizza in all of NYC.

While they serve a few platters, meatball heroes and salads, everyone comes for the pizzas: the thin crust pizza with endless toppings is unbeatable.

Jade Island
Open: *Mon to Thur 11:30am to 11:00pm, Fri 11:30am to midnight, Sat 12:30pm to midnight, Sun 12:30am to 11:00pm*
Address: *2845 Richmond Avenue*
Telephone: *718-761-8080*
Website: *jadeislandstaten.com*

This restaurant is quite the spectacle. It is a dark, spacious area, with a tropical motif. Staff wear Hawaiian shirts and serve sugary drinks.

On the small menu are Americanized Chinese staples. It is so over the top and goofy that you're bound to have a good time.

Lobster House Joe's
Address: *1898 Hyland Boulevard*
Hours: *Sun to Thur 11:00am to 10:00pm, Fri & Sat 11:00am to midnight*
Telephone: *718-667-0003*
Website: *lobsterhousesi.com*

When you're on an island of any sort, seafood always comes to mind when thinking of places to eat. Staten Island is no different, and a solid choice is Joe's Lobster House. With a relaxed casual environment, this restaurant serves seafood classics alongside decadent sweet desserts.

Maizal
Open: *Mon to Wed 5:00pm to 10:00pm; Thur & Sun 11:00am to 10:00pm, Fri & Sat 11:00am to 11:00pm*
Address: *990 Bay Street*
Telephone: *347-825-3776*
Website: *maizalrestaurant.com*

Staten Island has recently seen an influx of Mexican immigrants, which means one thing: great food. Popular items like fish tacos ($17) and Steak Ranchero ($23) are made with the famous Mole sauce from Mexico here.

Shopping

As well as being filled with museums, fantastic places to eat and amazing accommodation, New York City is also a world-class city for shopping. Many call it the shopping capital of the world, and you will find a multitude of places to shop – no matter your taste or budget.

There are a few shopping locations most visitors will be interested in: Times Square has big high-street brand names such as Disney, American Eagle and M&Ms.

Fifth Avenue is where you will find upmarket and designer brands such as Abercrombie, Apple, Tiffany and Co. and Dolce and Gabbana.

Finally, Madison Avenue is for true luxury brands such as Tom Ford, Missoni, Alexander McQueen, Hermès and Valentino.

As well as the aforementioned locations, large department stores such as Macy's and Bloomingdale's should be on shopaholics' must-do lists.

However, whether you are strolling through Chinatown or Queens, there is a shopping opportunity round every corner of this city.

This section lists some of the best shopping locations throughout NYC.

Bloomingdale's
Subway: 4/5/6/N/Q/R to 59 St – Lexington Av
Phone: 212-705-2000
Website: bloomingdales.com
Address: 59th Street and Lexington Avenue
Hours: Mon, Wed, Thur, Fri and Sat 10:00am to 9:30pm, Tues 10:00am to 8:30pm, Sun 11:00am to 9:00pm
This is one of the most famous department stores in NYC. Brands on offer here include ALLSAINTS, AQUA, Burberry, Michael Kors, MARC JACOBS, Ralph Lauren, as well as hundreds more. This is also the place to get the fashionable 'little' and 'medium brown bags' that so many carry around the city.

Whether it is high-end fashion, kids toys, home items, or luxury handbags, it is all at Bloomingdale's.

Apple Store
Subway: 4/5/6 to 59 St – Lexington, Av or N/Q/R to Lexington Av/59 St
Phone: 212-336-1440
Website: apple.com
Address: 767 5th Avenue
Hours: 24/7
Probably the most famous technology store in the world, the Apple Store's cubic entrance is recognized around the world. Inside, this is just like any other Apple Store where you can purchase products, get devices fixed at the Genius bar, and take tutorials and classes. The store is open 24 hours a day, 7 days a week.

Shopping

Macy's
Subway: A/C/E/1/2/3/B/D/F/V/N/Q/R/W to 34 Street
Phone: 212-695-4400
Website: macys.com
Address: 151 W 34th Street
Hours: Daily 10:00am to 10:00pm, except Sun when hours are 10:00am to 9:00pm.
Macy's is one of the most famous locations in New York, and up until 2009 this was the world's largest department store. Some of the brands in Macy's include Tommy Hilfiger, MAC, Martha Stewart Collection, 32 Degrees, Polo Ralph Lauren, Charter Club, Calvin Klein, Lacoste Home and Lancôme.

You can find vouchers online for a 10% discount off most of the store. Macy's goes full out for the Christmas season, so if you are visiting then, there's even more joy. The window displays year-round are something to be admired too.

Saks Fifth Avenue
Subway: B/D/F/V to 47-50/Rockefeller Center, or E/6 to 51 Street/Lexington Avenue
Phone: 212-753-4000
Website: saksfifthavenue.com
Address: 611 Fifth Avenue
Hours: Mon to Sat 9:30am to 9:00pm, Sun 10:00am to 8:30pm
Founded in 1898, Saks is steeped in history and is still one of the most visited and largest department stores in New York City. This high-end location features well-known designer brands such as Burberry, Diane von Furstenberg, Dolce & Gabbana, Givenchy, Jimmy Choo, Prada, and Valentino, amongst many others.

Barneys New York
Subway: 4/5/6 to 59 St – Lexington, Av or N/Q/R to Lexington Av/59 St
Phone: 212-826-8900
Website: barneys.com
Address: 660 Madison Avenue
Hours: Mon & Tues 10:00am to 8:00pm, Wed to Fri 10:00am to 9:00pm, Sat 10:00am to 8:00pm, and Sun 11:00am to 7:00pm
This is a relatively new addition to the department store line-up in NYC, having opened in 1993. The store is 275,000 square feet and is another high-end department store. Notable brands include Saint Lauren Paris, The Row, Burberry Prorsum and Thom Browne.

Hershey's Chocolate World
Subway: N/Q/R to 49 Street
Phone: 212-581-9100
Website: hersheys.com/visit-us/times-square.aspx
Address: 1593 Broadway
Hours: 9:00am to midnight daily
From the famous Hershey's chocolate kisses to jumbo candy bars, there is something for every chocolate fan at Hershey's.

Century 21
Subway: R to Cortlandt Street or 4/5 to Fulton Street
Phone: 212-227-9092
Website: c21stores.com
Address: 21 Dey Street
Hours: Mon to Wed 7:45am to 9:00pm, Thur & Fri 7:45am to 9:30pm, Sat 10:00am to 9:00pm, Sun 11:00am to 8:00pm
This New York City-based department store chain focuses on more affordable mid-range offerings than some of the aforementioned department stores. There are still many designer brands and Century 21 really focuses on providing big discounts, usually of 40% to 70% off the standard retail price. From clothing to housewares, and electronics to cosmetics, there is plenty of choice.

Maison Goyard
Subway: F to Lexington Av - 63 St
Phone: 212-813-0005
Website: goyard.com
Address: 20 E 63rd St
Hours: Mon, Tues, Wed, Fri 10:00am to 6:00pm, Thurs & Sat 10:00am to 7:00pm, Closed on Sun.
Until recently the only place you could purchase Goyard products was from small boutique sellers, but now Goyard has its own "maison" or home. Inside, it is Parisian-styled, yet with a distinct twist of New York elegance too. If designer handbags and luxury one-off accessories are your thing, then look no further.

M&M'S World
Subway: N/Q/R to 49 Street
Phone: 212-295-3850
Website: mmsworld.com
Address: 1600 Broadway
Hours: 9:00am to midnigiht daily
The same concept as the Hershey's store mentioned earlier, but for M&Ms. This store is directly opposite Hershey's. Personally, we prefer this store because it feels easier to move around as it is bigger. There is a wider variety of merchandise here too and (importantly) we prefer the taste of M&Ms chocolate.

Abercrombie & Fitch
Subway: E/M to 5 Av – 53 Street, or F to 57 Street
Phone: 212-306-0936
Website: abercrombie.com
Address: 720 Fifth Avenue
Hours: Mon to Sat 10:00am to 9:00pm, Sun 10:00am to 8:00pm.
Loved by teens and young twenty-somethings, Abercrombie has made its name through its athletic-fitted clothing that sticks to classic styles. The Fifth Avenue location is the company's flagship store which is famous for its high-priced clothing and attractive model-style employees. If you are looking for a bargain, visit the Fulton Street location, as this flagship store does not hold sales.

Shopping

Tiffany & Co.
Subway: E/M to 5 Av – 53 Street, or F to 57 Street
Phone: 212-755-8000
Website: tiffany.com
Address: 727 Fifth Avenue
Hours: Mon to Sat 10:00am to 7:00pm, Sun 12:00pm to 6:00pm
This is Tiffany's flagship retail location and has stood here since 1940. If diamonds are your best friend, you undoubtedly know that there is simply no better place to shop. As an added bonus, you can see the original Tiffany Diamond on display at this store.

The Strand Bookstore
Subway: 4/5/6/L/N/Q/R/L to Union Square
Phone: 212-473-1452
Website: strandbooks.com
Address: 828 Broadway
Hours: Mon to Sat 9:30am to 10:30pm, Sun 11:00am to 10:30pm
Booklovers need look no further than The Strand. Their collection of over 2.5 million items and 18 miles of bookshelves, means that you are bound to find something for the flight back home here. There is a rare books room filled with antique reads.

Chelsea Market
Subway: A/C/E to 14 Street
Phone: 212-652-2110
Website: chelseamarket.com
Address: 75 Ninth Avenue
Hours: Mon to Sat 7:00am to 2:00am, Sun 8:00am to 10:00pm. Individual shop hours may vary.
With the Highline passing through it, Chelsea Market is a must-see location which provides a sensory overload unlike anywhere else in the city. It is a food hall and shopping mall in one space, and is a joy to explore and some of the food is simply delightful.

Here, you forget that you are in a city with skyscrapers and feel like you are at a local market in any small town. Foods of NY Tours (www.foodsofny.com) runs paid-for tours of the market four times daily: these include tastes of some of the food on offer.

One of the most well-known locations inside the market is 'Artists & Fleas' where vendors sell handmade crafts, antiques, vintage clothing, jewelry and more.

The Independent Guide to New York City 95

Nightlife

Known as the city that never sleeps, NYC has plenty to offer during the evening. Whether you want a casual drink, a club to party the night away, live music or theatre and musical performances, there is something for every type of night owl. This section lists our favorite locations to spend an evening out in the city.

Bars/Lounges/Pubs/Clubs

Upstairs at the Kimberly Rooftop Bar and Lounge
Subway: 6 to 51 Street or E/M to Lexington Av/53 St
Phone: 212-702-1600
Website: upstairsnyc.com
Address: 145 E 50th St
Hours: Mon 5:00pm to midnight, Tues & Wed 5:00pm to 1:00am, Thu & Fri 5:00pm to 2:00am, Sat 12:00pm to 2:00am, Sun 12:00pm to 11:00pm

This bar provides some fantastic views of Midtown Manhattan and the famous Chrysler building from the 30th story. There are indoor and outdoor areas, and the bar serves small bites, as well as alcoholic and non-alcoholic beverages. This place oozes chic.

The dress code requires business casual dress, with no sneakers, caps or flip flops accepted. Signature cocktails run about $18, glasses of wine are $15 to $22, sides and sliders are $9 to $24.

The 13th Step
Subway: 6 to Astor Place
Phone: 212-228-8020
Website: nycbestbar.com
Address: 149 2nd Ave
Hours: Daily 11:30am to 4:00am

This huge bar has a college-like vibe to it, and therefore is very popular with the younger crowd. If you're a sports fan, like beer pong, and like a frat-like atmosphere, this may just be the perfect place for you.

Cocktails are much more affordable than at high-end bars, and regular happy hours and daily specials means you can get beers as low as $1 and shots from $4. Mixed drinks are $7, making this a bargain place to drink. The bar food is cheap and plentiful too.

Nightlife

Dive Bar
Subway: 1/2/3 to 96 Street
Phone: 212-749-4358
Website: divebarnyc.com
Address: 732 Amsterdam Ave
Hours: Daily 11:30am to 4:00am
A good local's joint with a large choice of beers, as well whiskeys/scotches, and good bar food. The staff are friendly and the atmosphere is great. This is a great place to hang out for a few hours, and sports games are often shown too. Despite its name, this isn't your typical 'dive bar' and the quality of service, drink and food is pretty great!

Le Bain
Subway: A/C/E to 14 St
Phone: 212-645-7600
Website: standardhotels.com/new-york/features/le-bain
Address: 444 W 13th Street
Hours: Closed Mon & Tue. Wed to Fri 10:00pm to 4:00am, Sat 2:00pm to 4:00am, Sun 2:00pm to 3:00am.
This bar/club combo features indoor and outdoor areas, with three hot tubs in total (one inside, two outside) which are open during the summer season. It is located on the top floor of The Standard High Line hotel. The crowd is generally very friendly, and who wouldn't be when there's a crêpe stand on the dance floor? The views are great from this rooftop location.

Mixed drinks are $14 here. Bring a bathing suit/shorts if you fancy swimming.

Cielo
Subway: A/C/E to 14 St
Phone: 646-543-8556
Website: cieloclub.com
Address: 18 Little W 12th St
Hours: Tues to Sun 10:00pm to 4:00am. Closed on Mon.
If you're a fan of techno, electronic and house music, this is the place for you. The club's sound system is one of the best in NYC. Cielo is, however, quite small as far as clubs go, and the cover charge can be high – ask before getting in line. Get a guest DJ, though, and the atmosphere can make for an unforgettable night out.

Live Music

Madison Square Garden
Subway: 1/2/3/A/C/E to 34 St – Penn Station
Phone: 212-749-4358
Website: thegarden.com
Address: 4 Pennsylvania Plaza
This is perhaps NYC's most famous multi-purpose venue, showing sports, as well as live concerts with a capacity of 20,000 people. Conveniently located in the heart of Manhattan, and with good transportation links, this is the place of choice for major artists when playing in the city.

Bowery Ballroom
Subway: B/D to Grand Street; F/J/M/Z to Essex/Delancey Street
Phone: 212-260-4700
Website: boweryballroom.com
Address: 6 Delancey Street
Many say this is the perfect-sized venue in New York, not too small but big enough to get great artists to host here. There are three levels to this venue providing different atmospheres, and levels of intimacy. This is one of our favorite venues in the city.

Mercury Lounge
Subway: F to 2nd Avenue or Delancey Street
Phone: 212-260-4700
Website: mercuryloungenyc.com
Address: 217 E Houston St
This is a great place for up and coming bands, and with a capacity of only 250 people, it is small and intimate. Ticket and drink prices are generally affordable by New York standards.

Irving Plaza
Subway: N/Q/R/4/5/6/L to Union Square
Phone: 212-777-6800
Website: venue.irvingplaza.com
Address: 17 Irving Place
This venue is well located and is a decent size. The sound system is good but it should be noted that the entire venue is standing room with no seats, which may be a problem for some. Some of the greatest acts of all-time have played here including U2, Eric Clapton and the Beastie Boys. This is another of our favorite venues in town.

Theater

A visit to NYC would not be complete without taking in one of the stunning productions on Broadway.

Whether it is a musical, historical drama or a thriller, there is a show for everyone. Off-Broadway productions are also available, but here we will focus on some of the top shows in the city at the moment.

Buying tickets:
To book theater tickets, you can either do so in advance over the phone or online, in person at the box office or you can visit one of the numerous ticket resellers.

If there is a show that you absolutely MUST see, the best option is to book online where you can often choose specific seats and have an idea of what your view of the stage will be like.

Discounted last-minute tickets:
If you can wait until you are in NYC, you can get great deals on many Broadway shows by visiting one of the TKTS booths (www.tdf.org).

The website will give you an idea of what tickets are currently on sale at the booths so you can have an idea of what shows regularly have discounted tickets. A TKTS app with live availability is also available. You cannot get these tickets online or over the phone, but only in person at the TKTS booths.

TKTS sells tickets for major shows at up to 50% off the regular price on the day of performance. There are three locations: Times Square, South Street Seaport and Downtown Brooklyn. The Times Square location is generally the busiest. Check online for opening times and get there early (before opening) to get the best choice of tickets.

Aladdin
Subway: 1/2/3/7/A/C/E/N/Q/R/S to Times Square
Phone: 866-870-2717
Website: aladdinthemusical.com
Address: New Amsterdam Theatre, 214 West 42nd Street
Disney's hit movie is now playing on Broadway! With rave reviews from critics, a hilarious genie and incredible sets, this is one show that is sure to spellbind the whole family.

The Phantom of the Opera
Subway: A/C/E to 42 St - Port Authority Bus Terminal
Phone: 212-239-6200
Website: thephantomoftheopera.com
Address: The Majestic Theatre, 247 West 44th Street
Andrew Lloyd Webber's hit musical is the longest-running on Broadway, and over 30 years later this stunning masterpiece entrances audiences young and old. The costumes are stunning, the story and score unforgettable, and the set changes have to be seen to be believed.

The Book of Mormon
Subway: C/E/1 to 50 St or N/Q/R to 49 St
Phone: 212-560-2197
Website: bookofmormonbroadway.com
Address: Eugene O'Neill Theatre, 230 W 49th Street
Winner of 9 Tony awards, including for Best Musical, The Book of Mormon is based on the Latter Day Saint's religious book and first opened in 2011. Since then it has made millions laugh.

Nightlife

Wicked
Subway: C/E/1 to 50 St
Phone: 212-586-6510
Website: wickedthemusical.com
Address: The Gershwin Theatre, 222 W 51st Street
This spellbinding musical retells the story behind the Wicked Witch of the West from "The Wizard of Oz". Through this funny and elaborate journey, we discover why she acts the way she does. Be prepared for beautiful costumes, elaborate sets and incredibly memorable musical numbers in one of the best shows to have ever hit Broadway.

Chicago
Subway: N/Q/R to 49 St or C/E to 50 St
Phone: 212-239-6200
Website: chicagothemusical.com
Address: The Ambassador Theatre, 219 W 39th Street
The longest-running American musical in Broadway history, running for over 20 years, Chicago is incredible. This satirical musical retells the story of celebrity criminals and the justice system.

The Lion King
Subway: 1/2/3/7/N/Q/R/S to Times Square – 42 St
Phone: 212-869-0550
Website: lionking.com
Address: The Minskoff Theatre, 200 W 45th St
Disney's 'The Lion King' retells the story of the hit movie through stunning animal puppets, incredible singing, and sets which transport you to East Africa. The show is the top-earning title in box-office history, having raked in over $6 billion in worldwide ticket sales.

Hamilton
Subway: A/C/E to 42 St - Port Authority Bus Terminal
Phone: 212-221-1211
Website: hamiltonbroadway.com
Address: Richard Rodgers Theatre, 226 W 46th St
This musical from Lin-Manuel Miranda retells the story of Alexander Hamilton, one of the founding fathers of the USA. With a unique score with samples from Notorious B.I.G., this is a patriotic show that has cemeted its spot as a Broadway classic. Tickets are extremely hard to secure.

Harry Potter and the Cursed Child
Subway: A/C/E to 42 St - Port Authority Bus Terminal
Phone: 877-250-2929
Website: harrypottertheplay.com
Address: The Lyric Theatre, 214 W 43rd St
This show is a masterpiece. With great acting, a fantastic storyline, incredible sets and magical special effects, Potter fans should not miss out on the opportunity of a lifetime to see what happened to 'The Boy Who Lived' after the movies and books. The story is split into 2 separate performances.

Chapter Nine | Seasonal Events

Seasonal Events

No matter what time of the year you visit, there is always something different and unique going on in the city. Here we cover some of our favorite events. Dates listed are for the next edition at the time of publication.

January
New York Boat Show – January 23rd to 27th, 2019
For over 100 years people have been coming to New York City for the best in boating and fishing equipment. See hundreds of boats, yachts, canoes, and other watercraft and equipment. Participants can also attend workshops and seminars about nautical topics given by some of the top experts in the business. Tickets are $16 for adults.

Winter Antiques Show – January 18th to 27th, 2019
Every winter, over 70 exhibitors come to New York City to display their best antiques from Antiquity to the present. Pieces from America, England, Europe, and Asia are represented at this fair. The entrance price is $25. The fair can be accessed by taking the 4 or 6 to 68th St – Hunter College

Lunar New Year Parade & Festival – February 5th, 2019
Celebrate the Year of the Pig in 2019 with parades of dancers, dragons, lanterns, and Chinese culture in Chinatown. You can find the parade traveling down Mott St., under the Manhattan Bridge, and up to Forsyth St. in Lower Manhattan. After the parade, enjoy some Chinese food or shopping in Chinatown. Get there on the Metro using the N, R, Q, 6, J, or Z train to Canal Street, or the B or D train to Grand St.

February
Westminster Dog Show – February 11th and 12th, 2019
Day or night you can see hundreds of different breeds of dog competing for Best in Show at the 140th Westminster Dog Show. Events during the day take place at The Piers 92/94, (711 12th Ave at 55th Street & West Side Highway). In the evening, they take place at Madison Square Garden, located at West 33rd Street & 7th Avenue. To get to Madison Square Garden on the subway take the 1, 2, 3, A, C, or E to 34th St/Penn Station.

March
New York City St. Patrick's Day Parade – March 17th
Celebrate over 250 years of Irish culture in New York City at the St. Patrick's Day Parade. Watch as over 100,000 people march down 5th Avenue showing Irish pride with bands, bagpipes, and traditional dancing. Afterwards, you can grab a pint at many of the Irish bars in the city. The parade starts at 11:00am at 44th St and 5th Avenue and continues to the Irish Historical Society at 79th St.

Seasonal Events

Macy's Flower Show – March 25th to April 8th, 2018
Head to the Macy's in Herald Square in March to see the store transformed into a garden. Flowers from all over the world are arranged and displayed by some of the world's best. Take in all the beauty during normal business hours. Entrance is free, but we're sure Macy's won't mind if you also make a few purchases in-store. The quickest way to get there is to hop on the D, F, N, Q, or R train to 34th St. – Herald Square.

April

New York International Auto Show – April 19th to 28th, 2019
The New York Auto Show started in 1900 and today displays over 1,000 cars and trucks, giving audiences their first glimpses at the newest cars, as well as concept designs. 2016 prices were $17 for adults & $7 for children. Get there on the subway by taking the 7 train to 34th St/11th Ave.

Tribeca Film Festival – April 17th to 28th, 2019
Enjoy artist talks, films, and other informative sessions about film and culture at the Tribeca Festival in Lower Manhattan. See the latest movies, many of which you cannot see anywhere else in a theater. Enjoy talks by some of the greatest actors, directors, and cinema scholars. Prices range from $10 to $35 depending on the event.

**Cherry Blossom Festival at Brooklyn Botanic Garden –
April 28th & 29th, 2018 / April 27th & 28th, 2019**
Also called Sakuri Matsuri, the cherry blossom festival includes events and performances about Japanese culture. You can also see the hundreds of cherry trees planted in the garden in full bloom. Prices are $30 for adults and $25 for students and seniors - under 12s go free. There are multiple entrances to the Botanic Garden but the 2 or 3 train to Eastern Parkway; B, Q, or S to Prospect Park; or the 4 or 5 will get you to the garden.

May

NYCxDESIGN – May 11th to 23rd, 2018
If you have an eye for good design, then come see the best of New York City in May. Spread across the city at over 100 venues, over 200 events are organized to showcase graphic design, architecture, furniture design, urban design, fashion, and more through exhibitions, talks, trade shows, and open studios. Most events are free to attend. Check the website for more specifics about locations.

TD Five Boro Bike Tour – May 6th, 2018 / May 5th, 2019
If you are adventurous or athletic, you can travel 40 miles across all five boroughs in one day. The tour starts in Lower Manhattan and ends with a trip on the Staten Island Ferry. You can join over 30,000 other cyclists on car-free roads all across New York City.

**Ninth Avenue International Food Festival –
May 19th & 20th, 2018 / May 18th & 19th, 2019**
Usually taking place in the third weekend in May, the Ninth Avenue International Food Festival offers hundreds of different styles and types of food, from savory to sweet, and from all around

the world. The festival is free to the public and takes place on 9th Avenue from 42nd St to 57th St. Take an empty stomach to the 42nd St – Port Authority stop on the A, C, or E train.

June

Museum Mile Festival – June 12th, 2018
New York City has some of the best museums in the world. You can visit many of them along Museum Mile, an area along 5th Avenue from 82nd St. to 105th St. On one day in June you can visit The Metropolitan Museum of Art, The Neue Galerie, The Guggenheim, Cooper Hewitt, The Africa Center, The Jewish Museum, Museum of the City of New York, and El Museo del Barrio for free. Enjoy car-free streets, live music, and art in the streets along with all the free museums. Get on the 4, 5 or 6 train to 86th St. to enjoy all the free culture.

River to River Festival – June 18th to 28th, 2018
The River to River Festival takes place in Lower Manhattan and on Governors Island. It is an arts and music festival providing access to dance, music, art, and new media. Seminars are held that include topics about creativity and architecture. Governor's Island can be accessed by a ferry ride across the East River.

July

Macy's Fourth of July Fireworks – July 4th, 2018 / July 4th, 2019
Celebrate the independence of the USA in the biggest city in the country. The fireworks display in New York City is huge and is broadcast to viewers all over the USA. Past musical guests have included Beyoncé and Katy Perry. Macy's sets off the fireworks from 6 barges in the East River. The best places to see the fireworks are in the parks and viewing areas along the East River in Lower Manhattan and Brooklyn.

August

US Open (Tennis) – August 27th to September 11th, 2018
Travel to Queens on the 7 train to Mets – Willets Pont Station to see tennis greats battle for the final Grand Slam tournament of the year.

September

Electric Zoo Festival – August 31st to September 2nd, 2018
The Electric Zoo Festival brings over 100,000 people from around the world to Roosevelt Island to listen and dance to some of the best electronic music and various sub-genres. If lights, dancing, and electronic beats are your idea of fun, you can get to Roosevelt Island by ferry, bus, or by walking across the footbridge. Tickets start at about $179.

Seasonal Events

Feast of San Gennaro – Dates to be confirmed
Celebrate hundreds of years of Italian culture in New York City in Little Italy for 11 days. Enjoy parades, concerts, and lots of food at the annual feast.

October

New York Comic-Con/Animé Festival – October 4th to 7th, 2018
See all things comic, animation, fantasy, and sci-fi related at New York Comic-Con in October. Enjoy fans in elaborate costumes as well as film screenings, booths, and panel talks by some of the world's best in the field. Take the 7 train to 34 St and 11 Ave to get there.

Open House New York Weekend – October 13th & 14th, 2018
Every October, for two days, you can see the best of New York City's architecture. Visit buildings across all five boroughs, many of which are usually closed to the public. Experience contemporary, historical, residential, and commercial architecture through visits, tours, talks, and other events celebrating the history of architecture in New York City.

NYC Village Halloween Parade – October 31st
In costume or not, enjoy all the wild and wacky Halloween fun in the West Village this year. The parade progresses along 6th Avenue from Spring Street to 16th Street. It starts around 7:00pm and ends around 11:00pm. Watch as Halloween's most creative puppets, bands, and dancers march in costume. Take the A, B, C, D, E, or F train to get to 6th Avenue in the West Village.

November

**TCS New York City Marathon –
November 4th, 2018 / November 3rd, 2019**
Join the thousands of runners as a participant or a spectator at the New York City Marathon. Spread across the five boroughs, the race is a 26.2-mile physical feat.

Radio City Christmas Spectacular – Dates to be confirmed
A trip to New York City would not be complete without a trip to see the world famous Rockettes kick and dance through the Christmas season. The show also includes dancing Santas, ballet, a Living Nativity, and (of course) lots of great music. Shows begin in mid-November and end in early January. Tickets range from about $50 to $300. Radio City Music Hall is located near Rockefeller Center and can be easily found at the 47-50th Sts – Rockefeller Center stop on the B, D, F, M line.

Rockefeller Center Tree Lighting – Dates to be confirmed
In late November, you can be a part of Christmas magic in New York City by attending the Rockefeller Center Tree Lighting. Enjoy the thousands of lights being switched on at the Rockefeller Center and get a kick start to the Christmas spirit with the famous ice skating rink and music performed by top acts.

Seasonal Events

Macy's Thanksgiving Day Parade – November 22nd, 2018 / November 28th, 2019
Starting at 9:00am, you can be along the route of one of the most famous parades in the Unites States. The best places to view the parade are along 6th Avenue from 38th Street to 59th Street, and along Central Park West from 59th Street to 77th Street. Look forward to the giant balloons and the elaborate floats filled with characters, singing, and dancing. Look out for many celebrity appearances and the beginning of Christmas season with Santa near the end of the parade. The event is free to the public. You can also see the balloons being inflated the night before.

The Nutcracker – Dates to be confirmed
Throughout late November and the month of December, you can experience the best of New York ballet in the form of the world famous *The Nutcracker*. The ballet comprises over 200 performers, and is sure to delight people of all ages with the lights, music, costumes, and dance. Tickets range from $75 to around $250. The ballet takes place in the David H. Koch Theater, a part of Lincoln Center. The 1 or 2 trains will get you to the Lincoln Center.

December

Times Square New Year's Eve – December 31st
Brave the New York City cold with thousands of other people to ring in the New Year in Times Square. Enjoy live music performed by many of the year's top artists. Watch as the famous Times Square ball drops and enjoy a kiss with a loved one to celebrate a new beginning and a new year.

Chapter Ten | Maps

Maps

The following pages include maps of New York City's Manhattan. The map gives you an overview of the city's areas with the most attractions. These maps are not designed to be used for walking directions, but instead to give you a general sense of where different areas of the city are located in relation to each other. Maps go from north (uptown) to south (downtown).

Maps

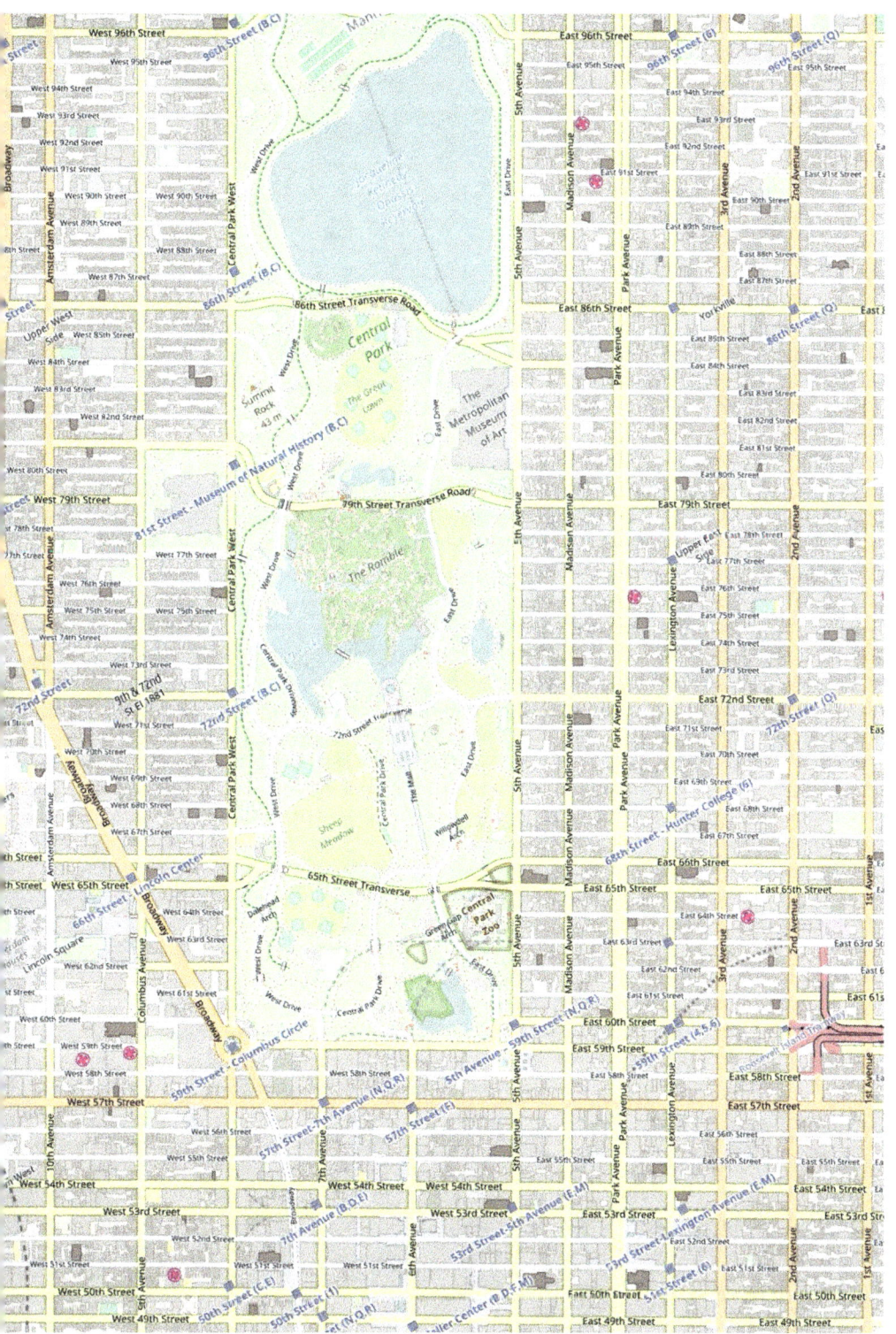

Maps

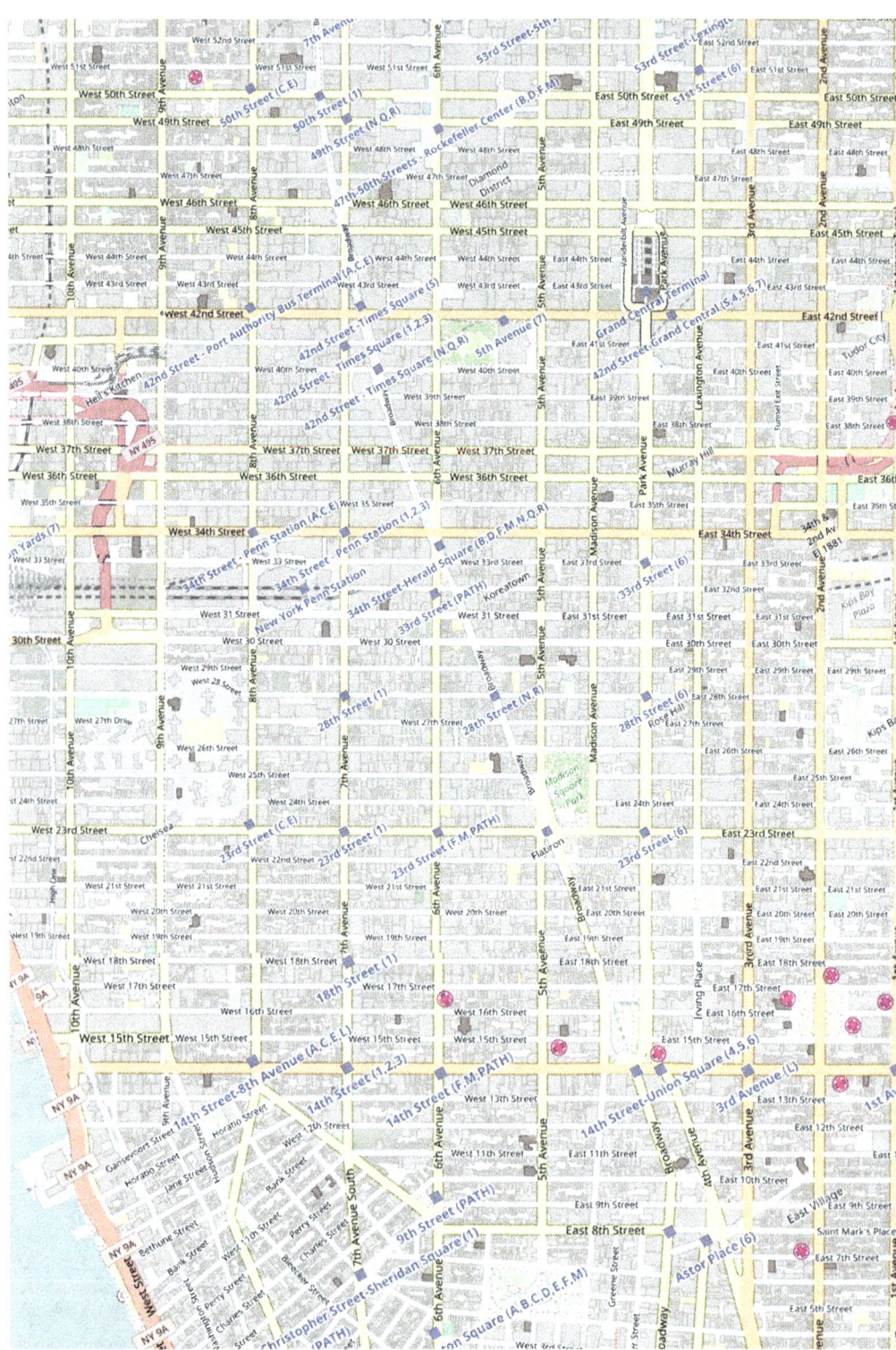

Maps

A Special Thanks

*If you have made it this far, thank you very much for reading everything.
We hope this guide will make a big difference to your trip to New York City!
Remember to take this guide with you whilst you are visiting this amazing city.*

If you have any questions or wish to contact us, visit independentguidebooks.com. If you have any corrections, feedback about any element of the guide, or a review of an attraction, hotel, area or restaurant – send us a message and we will get back to you.

We also encourage you to leave a review on the Amazon website, or wherever you have purchased this guide from. Your reviews make a huge difference in helping other people find this guide, and we really appreciate your help.

If you have enjoyed this guide, other travel guides in this series include:

- The Independent Guide to London
- The Independent Guide to Paris
- The Independent Guide to Hong Kong
- The Independent Guide to Tokyo
- The Independent Guide to Dubai
- The Independent Guide to Universal Orlando
- The Independent Guide to Disneyland
- The Independent Guide to Disneyland Paris
- The Independent Guide to Walt Disney World
- The Independent Guide to Universal Studios Hollywood
- Amazing London Walks (Self-Guided Walking Tours)

Have a fantastic time in New York City!

Photo Credits:
9/11 Memorial – Edward Stojakovic; ABC No Rio – 'The All-Nite Images' (Flickr); Alice's Tea Cup – Steve Isaacs; American Folk Art Museum – Edward Blake; American Museum of Natural History – Steeven Manon; Apollo Theater – Juan Puertas; Blue Note – Satish Krishnamurthy; Brooklyn Bridge – Daniel X. O'Neil; Brooklyn Museum – Kent Wang; Bronx Zoo – Steve Harrison; Bryant Park – John Gillespie; Central Park – 'Mariko' (Flickr); Charging Bull – Sam Valadi; Chelsea Market – Mark Johnson; Coney Island – Maelick (Flickr); Cotton Club – 'Dariorug' (Flickr user); Empire State Building – Ivo Jansch; Ess-A-Bagel – Jennifer Feuchter; Five Boro Bike Tour – 'dumbonyc' (Flickr); FlatIron building – John McKerrell; Freshkills Park – Kristine Paulus; Gramercy Tavern – 'london road' (Flickr); Grand Central – Eric Wüstenhagen; Guggenheim – Vincent Desjardins; Harlem YMCA – Stefano Brivio; Hershey's – Mrs. Gemstone; Highline – David Berkowitz; Highline Hotel – Highline hotel website; Joe's Pizza – Rob Young; Katz's Delicatessen – Shelley Panzarella; La Mela – Andres Moreira; Lincoln Center – Chun-Hung Eric Cheng; Lunar New York Parade – May S. Young; Macy's – Pete Bellis; Macy's Fireworks – Joseph Bylund; Macy's Thanksgiving Day Parade – Ben W; Madison Square Park and Gramercy Park– Jeffrey Zeldman; Mamoun's and Washington Square Hotel – Alan Turkus; Metropolitan Museum of Art – Monica Arellano-Ongpin; MoMA PS1 – Jeffrey Montes; Museum of Chinese in America – Monica Wong; Museum of Sex – Maju Rezende; Mustang Thakali Kitchen – Gary Stevens; New Museum – Franklin Heijnen; New York City Fire Museum – 'State Farm' (Flickr); New York Public Library – Melanzane1013 (Flickr user); Noguchi Museum – Shinya Suzuki; Peanut Butter & Co – Uri Baruchi; Pete's Tavern, The Odeon, Brandy Library, Feast of San Gennaro and McSorley's – 'Jazz Guy' (Flickr); Prospect Park – Allison Meier; Red Rooster – Maria Eklind; Rockefeller Center – Erik Drost; Russ and Daughters – Jeffrey Bary; Serendipity 3 – Ben W; Socrates Sculpture Park – Mike Boucher; St. Patrick's Cathedral – Ben Sutherland; Stonewall Inn – 'InSapphoWeTrust' (Flickr); South Street Seaport – Ana Paula Hirama; Tenement Museum – Tom Bastin; The Bowery Hotel – 'La Citta Vita' (Flickr); The Cornelia Street Café – Pieter Iserbyt; The Clositers – Laura Bittner; The Edgar Allan Poe Cottage – Shannon McGee; The Frick Collection – Rev Stan; The Halal Guys – Tal Atlas; The Meatball Shop – Davis Staedtler; The Standard High Line – Jessica Sheridan; The Waldorf Astoria – Chris Breeze; Times Square – Greg Knapp; Times Square New Years Eve – Anthony Quintano; Tom's Restaurant – GabboT (Flickr user); Tompkins Square Park – 'Jschauma' (Flickr); Top of the Rock – Alexandre Andre; Union Square Greenmarket – Stepan Roh; Washington Square Park – Doc Searls; and Williamsburg – Rasmus Zwickson. Cover credits: Statue of Liberty Big – Brooklyn Bridge – Andrés Nieto Porras; Manhattan Skyline – William Warby; NYC Cab – Pascal Subtil; Statue of Liberty – Marek Kubica; Times Square, Skyline small and Greenwich Village – Aurelien Guichard; Central Park – Doug Kerr; Hot dog cart - rollingrck; Tip jar - Dave Dugdale; JFK airport terminal – Eric Salard; Subway car interior - Mirage Clicks; Citibike – Omar Rawlings; Brooklyn Bridge with Skyline - Andres Nieto Porras; Times Square – Aurelien Guichard; Harlem Wall Mural – Karin; Gramercy Vintage Shop - Karen Horton; and Nuyorican Poets Cafe – Daniel X. O'Neil; subway entrance - Elvert Barnes; MOMA - alan huette; Rubin museum of art – S Pahkrin; Chelsea market - Shinya Suzuki; Bloomingdale's - chrisinphilly5448; apple store - Davis Staedtler; Saks Fifth Avenue - Brian Lauer; Barneys – Jim Henderson; Century 21 - John Wisniewski; Maison Goyard - goyard.com; M&M'S World - Wikimedia; Abercrombie - Rob Young; Tiffany – "SpeechRep"; The Strand Bookstore - Joe Loong; Upstairs NYC Bar - upstairsnyc.com; The 13th Step - nycbestbar.com; Dive Bar - Augusto P.; Le Bain - standardhotels.com; Cielo - cieloclub.com; Madison Square Garden - msg.com; Bowery Ballroom - Steven Pisano; Mercury Lounge - nycgo.com; Irving Plaza - Beyond My Ken; Westminster Dog Show - Terry Ballard; St. Patrick's Day - Charley Lhasa; Theatre shows - respective owners; Cherry Blossom Festival - Baldwin Saintilus; River to River Festival - Jebb; US Open Tennis - Steven Pisano; Halloween Parade - Joe Shlabotnik;

www.ingramcontent.com/pod-product-compliance
Lightning Source LLC
LaVergne TN
LVHW021943060526
838200LV00042B/1908